THE SWALLOWING WILDERNESS

THE SWALLOWING WILDERNESS

The Life of a Frontiersman: James Ohio Pattie

by

Stanton A. Coblentz

Thomas Yoseloff
New York • London

Thomas Yoseloff, *Publisher*
11 East 36th Street
New York 16, N.Y.

Thomas Yoseloff, Ltd.
123 New Bond Street
London W. 1, England

Printed in the United States of America

Contents

Contents

Introduction

JAMES OHIO PATTIE, frontiersman and explorer, is a character little known to the average reader of American history. Yet he had one of the strangest, most varied, and most adventurous careers in pioneering annals. It was in 1824 that he started westward from St. Louis in company with his father Sylvester; and it was not until 1830 that he returned to his old home in Kentucky, after wanderings that had taken him across prairies and deserts, up the gorges of untraveled streams, and over the ice and snow of unknown mountain passes.

During those nomadic six years he had frequent battles and as frequent friendly encounters with the Indians, whom he was able to observe in their aboriginal state. He faced death from wild beasts, from thirst and famine, from the craftiness of savages, the treachery of companions, and the hostility of nature. He threaded the Grand Canyon of the Colorado when its fame was still unsung. He saved himself from perishing in the desert, only to be thrown into prison in California; and helped to suppress a revolution against the man who had persecuted him. He journeyed up and down the coast, on horseback and by sailing vessel, and viewed the life of the ranches and missions; he suffered enormous losses and refused princely offers; he engaged in one or two romances or near romances with black-eyed señoritas; and ended by going to the city of Mexico to seek the redress for his injuries that the California authorities had denied him.

Here, it seems to me, are the materials for a human story of the first degree of interest. Here is a panorama so little explored as to be almost virgin territory; and here is, likewise, a first-hand glass with which to peer at a vanished America and to observe its inhabitants and their ways of thought and life. Yet the tale is hidden from the ordinary reader in rare and out-of-print books. The only complete source is *The Personal Narrative of James O. Pattie of Kentucky*, which, edited by Timothy Flint and published in 1831 by John H. Wood of Cincinnati, has been fully reprinted but twice: first, by Reuben G. Thwaites as Volume XVIII of his *Early Western Travels* (Cleveland, 1905); and, secondly, by R. R. Donnelley & Sons Company of Chicago, which in 1930 issued a private gift edition as one of their Lakeside Classics.

Chancing upon a copy of the latter reprint several years ago, I was struck with the possibilities of a modernized version of Pattie's story. For some time I allowed the idea to grow in my mind; and the more I thought about it, the more persuaded I became that an effort should be made to rescue the Patties from the near oblivion that had engulfed them. It seemed to me that a book should be written, based upon James Ohio's chronicle and yet relying upon supplementary sources in its delineation of the country and its people. I felt that certain gaps in the *Personal Narrative* should be bridged; that the whole deserved to be scrutinized anew, from the perspective of our own century; and that the significance of Pattie's journal and its value for our own day should be reappraised.

These are the thoughts that have led to my retelling of the story. As far as has seemed practicable, I have followed the course of James Ohio's own narrative; but I have taken the position of an independent observer looking down over the long reaches of a century and a third, and have not hesitated to reorganize the material when this appeared desirable. I have kept constantly in mind my aim to cover everything essential in Pattie's recital; I have sought to be true to the spirit of the man and the times; and I know that the fault has been mine alone if the report is not vital and interesting and does not offer valuable historical sidelights.

A word remains to be said as to the accuracy of the original journal. Some of Pattie's statements have been challenged by the western historian, H. H. Bancroft, who in Volume III of his *California* attacks James O. Pattie as "a self-conceited and quick-tempered boy, with a freedom of speech often amounting to insolence." And other authorities have expressed doubts as to some of the adventures on the ground of sheer incredibility. But incredibility in itself, it seems to me, is a poor objection; for the incredible was repeatedly happening among the pioneers of the New World. What could be more unbelievable, for example, than the conquest of Peru by Pizarro and his handful of adventurers, or than the passage of Lewis and Clark over the unknown continent to the Pacific, or than the grisly but well-authenticated experiences of the Donner party?

This much, I think, must be conceded: any man, writing a journal after six years of wanderings during which he made neither diary nor notes, will be guilty of some minor inaccuracies and possibly even of exaggerations that are not so much deliberate as due to the warping perspectives of time. But this does not necessarily mean that any major episodes have been distorted. We have, indeed, corroborating evidence in the

fact that some of the historical happenings Pattie records—
for example, the revolt of General Solis, and the overthrow
of President Guerrero of Mexico—are well known to have occurred. Certain of his specific statements on more obscure
matters—such as his reference to the arrival of the United
States vessel *Franklin* in the harbor of San Diego under Captain John Bradshaw and the escape of the latter under gunfire
after being detained on a charge of smuggling—have likewise
been confirmed from other sources, despite some confusion as
to minor data. Or to take some further details as a check on
Pattie's basic reliability—minute and unimportant details,
such as could not readily be obtained from a secondary source
—the narrator states that while in San Diego he met three
ship captains, whose names he recalls as Seth Rogers, Aaron
W. Williams, and H. Cunningham. All three, I find, are mentioned in Bancroft's *Marine List,* 1825–1830 (*California,*
Volume III), but "W. Cunningham" is named instead of
"H. Cunningham"—a minor variation such as anyone's memory could commit, though it may not be an actual error, since
Bancroft elsewhere refers to the shipmaster as "W. H. Cunningham."

If evidence such as this were not sufficient—and other ex-
amples might be cited, including the convincing circumstance
that Pattie's visit to Mexico is mentioned to the Department
of State at Washington in letters from the American legation—
we have the fact that most, if not all, of the unique customs
that Pattie describes have been verified by other writers. One
such is the strange but amply attested practice of bull-bear
fighting in California. And another is the spectacle of bull-
fighting both in California and in Mexico, including the specific features depicted by Pattie, such as the incidental slaughter of horses and the discharge of small "rockets" from the
infuriated animals ("firecrackers" might be a more accurate
term, though in any case the meaning is clear).

One impressive question nevertheless remains unanswered. Milo Milton Quaife, in his introduction to the Lakeside edition of the *Personal Narrative*, has put the matter plainly and simply:

> The student who seeks to follow Pattie in his wanderings is perplexed by the almost total absence of names which will serve to identify his companions. Newly returned from the scene of his adventures, he could not possibly have remembered the experiences described and at the same time have forgotten the names of his companions in peril. Why then did he, with undeviating purpose, refrain from supplying them?

A tentative solution has been supplied by Joseph J. Hill, of the Bancroft Library of the University of California, who identifies Pattie's Gila and Colorado River expeditions (although not positively) with the expeditions of 1826–27 of Robidoux and Young. Hill suggests that Pattie played but a subordinate part in these expeditions; that though he actually experienced the adventures recorded in his journal, he depicts himself in more conspicuous roles than the facts would warrant. "For this reason," Quaife in his introduction summarizes the matter, "he could not supply the names of his companions, or even identify the expeditions he had accompanied, since to do so would render him liable to prompt exposure by those who had shared his adventures."

All this, it seems to me, is plausible. It is, of course, no palliation of the narrator's vainglory to say that this quality has been shared by many and many another autobiographer. Nor is it relevant to add that it makes the storyteller appear the more human. The important point is that it does not detract from the interest or the general reliability of the record.

In considering the matter of reliability, furthermore, we must not overlook the attitude of Pattie's contemporaries, who knew him best and were in the most strategic position to judge his character and sift his statements. It is notable that these men, with their wide personal knowledge of the west, seem to have suffered from no doubts. Thus the Reverend Timothy Flint, a man of education and experience, editor of *The Western Monthly Review*, and author of some of our most valuable accounts of frontier life, has this to say in his preface to the original edition:

> For, in the literal truth of the facts, incredible as some of them may appear, my grounds of conviction are my acquaintance with the Author, the impossibility of inventing a narrative like the following, the respectability of his relations, the standing which his father sustained, the confidence reposed in him by the Hon. J. S. Johnston, the very respectable senator in Congress from Louisiana, who introduced him to me, the concurrent testimony of persons now in this city, who saw him at different points in New Mexico, and the reports, which reached the United States during the expedition, of many of the incidents here recorded.

At this late date, it appears to me, it would be as rash to question the basis for this judgment as it would be difficult to quarrel with Flint's further remarks:

> The journalist sees in these pages a legitimate descendant of those western pioneers, the hunters of Kentucky, a race passing unrecorded from history. The pencil of biography could seize upon no subject of higher interest. With hearts keenly alive to the impulses of honor and patriotism, and the charities of kindred and friends; they possessed spirits impassible to fear, that no form of suffering or death could daunt; and frames for strength and endurance, as if ribbed with brass and sinewed with steel. For them to traverse wide deserts, climb mountains, swim rivers, grapple with the grizzly bear, and encounter the savage, in a sojourn in the wilderness of years, far from the abodes of civilized men, was but a spirit-stirring and holiday mode of life.

Having seen the Patties and their comrades through the eyes of a contemporary, let us conclude with the verdict of a historian of the twentieth century. The following is from Robert Glass Cleland's *From Wilderness to Empire: A History of California* (revised edition, 1959):

> The critical historian may point out discrepancies in dates, confusion in routes, and misstatement of fact; but the tale remains a classic adventure story of the West—an epic saga of the Mountain Men.

THE
SWALLOWING
WILDERNESS

1

Sylvester and James Ohio Pattie

ON THE morning of March 27, 1828, eight Americans were led under guard into the office of José María de Echeandía, the Mexican governor at San Diego. They were a disheveled lot. Their clothes, encrusted with the grime and dust of thousands of miles, were little more than hanging rags. Their beards were long, unkempt, and tangled, and stained in some cases with tobacco juice; the skin of their hands and necks was covered with hundreds of little red marks, made by sand fleas in the guardhouse where they had spent the night; specks of blood oozed through the shirts recently given them at one of the missions.

The governor cast them a stare of hostile appraisal. His temper, aggravated by poor health, was not at all helped by his recollection of his meeting the year before with another American, Jedediah Smith, who had entered California illegally and under false excuses.

"Señores, who are you?"

The leader of the party, a lean, worn, and grizzled man in his late forties, came forward and, in a faltering Spanish, introduced himself as Sylvester Pattie. He pleaded that he and his followers had suffered long and cruel adventures in the desert and had come to California as the only alternative to perishing. They wished merely food, water, horses, and equipment and were eager to return to their own country. After fumbling about in his soiled hunting jacket, Sylvester produced a grimy old paper which he claimed to be a passport issued to him several years before by Governor Bartolome Baca of Santa Fe.

Echeandía, remembering the claim of Jedediah Smith that he, too, had come for food, water, equipment, and horses, scowled and snatched up the paper; and after a hasty glance denounced it as a forgery and tore it to bits. A suspicion, growing in his mind ever since he had first heard of the arrival of the suspicious-looking strangers at the Dominican mission of Santa Catalina on March 8, now seemed to be confirmed. These rogues were really spies for the Spaniards, who had never given up hope of bringing the recently liberated Californians back beneath their yoke. The ruffians had been exploring the defenseless parts of the frontier, so as to bear information to the enemy, who might strike back with their troops!

Not unnaturally Echeandía's reaction was severe. "To the guardhouse with them all!" he snapped at the soldiers who stood by with muskets pointed. And disregarding the agitated protests of the prisoners, who had confidently expected to be set free, he ordered each of the suspects to a separate cell, so as to prevent them from plotting together.

This episode, which was to mark the end of the trail for Sylvester Pattie and would introduce a long, grim interlude between adventures for his son James Ohio, came as the climax of years of wandering among strange men and in strange lands—years of fighting, trapping, and exploring, illuminated by episodes as hectic and colorful as any ever recorded in the annals of the west.

It had all begun tamely enough in June 1824. It was then that the elder Pattie, grieved by the recent death of his wife and unable to care properly for the eight children who were growing up wild about him, sold the saw and grist mill which he had been operating on the Gasconade about a hundred miles above St. Louis, and sent his sons and daughters to live with various relations. Though he was beyond forty, the spirit of adventure was still hot in his blood; he was a veteran of the Indian wars, had fought the redmen throughout much of Kentucky and Tennessee, and had distinguished himself by his bravery when, in command of a detachment at the fort of Cap au Gris on the Mississippi, he had slipped on the uniform of a dead Englishman, passed by night through the enemy lines, and summoned aid to save the beleaguered garrison. Even now, with the daring of a younger man, he dreamed of an untraveled wilderness of mountains, streams, forests, and teeming wildlife; and, gripped by impatience at a settled existence, aimed to set out on a trapping expedition into the little-known reaches of the Upper Missouri. Such expeditions in Pattie's day were much talked of, though they could be accomplished only by hardy and experienced backwoodsmen.

At this time his son James Ohio, if we can accept his own testimony, was twenty years old (though some of the statements in his journal would indicate that he was quite a bit younger). Whatever his age, he was still at school, receiving the rude but by no means negligible education of the day (an education that was to play a valuable part years later, when he came to write his *Personal Narrative*). Sylvester, with fatherly solicitude, wished him to remain at school, but Jim had different ideas. In his blood, too, was the spirit of the wanderer; he, too, had been trained in the lore of the backwoods; he, too, knew what it meant to roam all day, rifle on shoulder, and to face the challenge of the wilderness, and defy its dangers. And so, when he learned of the projected expedition, he had no desire to remain dully behind; the father knew no peace until he gave the son permission to join the company.

The actual group, which left St. Louis on a June day of 1824, contained but five men, including the two Patties, and was served by ten horses, which lumbered forward laden with equipment, including guns and ammunition, traps and trapping gear, blankets, knives, and tomahawks. The men hoped that as they proceeded, they would gain recruits to their party, but they hoped in vain: they could find no one who was not intimidated by the trials and perils of the adventure.

It may be that fate sometimes casts her shadow before her. The first incidents of the journey, while not spectacular, might have been taken by a superstitious onlooker to be sinister omens. To begin with, one of the small company of five took sick and had to be left behind at Charaton, the furthermost village on the western frontier. Then at the trading establishment near the site of the present city of Council Bluffs on the Missouri, the remaining four were turned back. Pattie's story is that the commanding officer at the post demanded to see their license for trading with the Indians; and, finding that they had none and had not even heard that one was necessary, refused to let them proceed. Whether or not this version is correct—and it may be that an officious or corrupt commandant made demands unauthorized by law—we may accept Pattie's statement that the company could not advance beyond Council Bluffs. Nor need we question his word that at this point one of the four members of the party in discouragement forsook his comrades.

The remaining three, clearly, were too few to face the hardships of the proposed expedition—the possible bouts with wild beasts, the brushes with Indians, the peril to all should one of the trio become disabled or seriously ill. At this crisis, however, they were not without resources. Though disheartened, they exchanged their surplus arms for merchandise, shifted their destination from the Upper Missouri to New Mexico, and set out to find the followers of Sylvester Pratte, the son of the noted General Bernard Pratte. The younger Pratte was a man of twenty-five, who, like his father before him, was active in the fur trade. Shortly after leaving St. Louis, the Patties had met Pratte at a trading post on the Missouri and had learned that he had gathered a large company for a trapping expedition to New Mexico. The best hope for the Patties, therefore, was to join Pratte's group.

But how could they find Pratte? The difficulty may have seemed imposing but was not really very great. On the vast open reaches of the prairie, where white travelers were rare as ships on an unexplored ocean, a large band of trappers, with their mules and horses, could not pass without setting up dust clouds visible for long distances. To a native scout, who would pick up information at various villages, it would be little more than a routine matter to locate Pratte and his men. And Sylvester Pattie, in return for the promise of a suitable consideration, was able to obtain such a scout.

One evening at sunset after a hard, forced march, during which they were reduced to using buffalo dung in the Indian style for cooking, they arrived at a spot on the River Platte where a large party was encamped and where, with shouts of joy, they recognized some of Pratte's men. That same evening the scout, refusing the use of a horse, set out on the return trip to his own people. And meanwhile the Patties were enthusiastically received by Pratte and his comrades, many of whom had served as rangers under Sylvester.

For four days they remained in camp by the Platte, hunting for antelope and deer, whose skins they dressed for moccasins. Then suddenly Sylvester was projected into an unexpected position. He was approached by Pratte with the request that he take command of the company—which, by subsequent roll call, was found to consist of a hundred and sixteen men. One's natural assumption, though the *Personal Narrative* is silent on this point, is that the twenty-five-year-old Pratte was finding the rude, hard-bitten men unruly, if not unmanageable, and felt the need of an older and more experienced guiding hand. In any case Pattie, as a man known and respected by most of the party, was a natural choice as leader.

Having accepted the appointment, he made out a list of the names of the entire company, divided it into four messes, and directed each mess to furnish two men to stand guard by turns at night. He then took stock of the common resources, which he found to contain three hundred mules in addition to some horses, including a hundred pack animals laden with baggage. He then gave orders for the men to get under way, and on the morning of August 6 they set out along the Platte, which at this point was a clear, shallow stream flowing between high banks fringed with willows and cottonwoods. The caravanlike band, as it moved forward, made an impressive sight, the mules plodding in long, slow files, with drooping necks, and tails swishing amid clouds of dust. A scattering of horses, with their riders, moved back and forth more agilely; while far along the flanks of the party the mounted guards deployed, sometimes hidden beyond rises in the land, but usually remotely visible. By waving their hats, or by pistol shots if they were out of sight, these scouts were to give warning of Indians.

At last the Patties were truly launched upon their adventure.

2

Adventures among the Indians

DURING THEIR years in the wilderness and amid their innumerable encounters with the Indians, the Patties were like the typical white intruder in their attitude toward the native: self-confident, arrogant, at times condescending, on occasion kindly and considerate, but often violently hostile. Already in the Patties' day the white man had ravaged much of the territory over which they traveled, and for this they often suffered cruelly. But in places they saw the Indian still in his native state and still with no ill will against the invader.

Even before they joined Pratte's party, their experiences with the Indians had begun. One day they held a friendly conference with a Pawnee chief who smoked a pipe of peace while a tribesman held the bowl of the pipe. The smoking was a religious ceremonial, in which the chief filled his mouth with the smoke, then puffed it over the chests of the white men, then on to his own chest, then upward to where he supposed the Great Spirit to be, in order that this powerful being might grant the travelers many fat buffaloes and other necessities. From this chief they recieved a stick scrawled with curious characters, and were told to give the stick to any of his warriors whom they might meet—this would insure their being treated kindly.

Their next contact with the Indians, which occurred after they had joined Pratte, was likewise amicable—at least, in the beginning. It was at a village of the Pawnee Loups, where the chief received them hospitably and gave them all the provisions they wished. He was not, however, a complete stranger to the white world; he was one of the fortunate few who had traveled all the way to the chief white village, known as Washington, and there he had been astonished to learn that the whites were not a small tribe like his own, but were "numberless as the spires of grass on the prairies." But what was it that had most surprised him? It was that the white men had bullets as large as his head, which they fired through guns as big as logs.

For five days the company remained at the Indian village, where they bought six buffalo skins and some horses and had a chance to learn something of Indian warfare. A war party came in triumphantly from a raid on some hostile red men, four of whom they had scalped, while they had seized twenty horses. Next day they held a celebration, in which the braves strutted in headdresses of eagles' feathers, necklaces of bears' and panthers' claws, and robes of the skin of the puma, the grizzly, and the wolf. Painted with elaborate care, the warriors stalked forth with their guns, their war clubs, and their bows and arrows; tied the captured scalps to the top of a tall pole; and began shouting, singing, and dancing about the pole with exultant capers. We can picture the tumult and confusion from Jim's statement that "a recruit of fiends from the infernal regions could hardly have transcended them in genuine diabolical display."

For three days the pandemonium continued. But even after the excitement had begun to pall and the warriors had pulled down the poles and given the scalps to the women, they took the relics back again, and began kicking and throwing them to one another in a kind of a football, while growling and muttering their anger and scorn.

Meanwhile one incident had particularly impressed the Patties. Along with the captured horses and the scalps of their enemies, the war party had brought in a small boy, whose mother they had scalped. Why had they taken this tiny prisoner? They could not say—in their warfare it was usual to kill men, women, and children alike. But the sparing of the child's life represented no act of mercy. The victim was bound hand and foot, and fed barely enough to keep him alive; and after several days, when the commotion over the scalps had ended, he was taken to the Medicine Lodge, where the incantations to the Great Spirit were made. With horror, as they stared at the pitiable pain-stricken little face, the whites realized that the Pawnees were preparing to sacrifice the boy.

How could they save his life? As the most likely way, they offered to buy him. But the chief scowled his displeasure. What! If his friends saw a young rattlesnake in their path, would they spare it just because it was not big enough to bite? But the boy, protested the Patties, was not a rattlesnake; if brought up among the Pawnees, he would grow to be a brother to them.

Not so! denied the chief. He had made exactly this experiment, and the children of other tribes had only caused trouble when they grew up. It was like hatching the eggs of the partridge: you might raise the young birds carefully in cages, but would they show any gratitude? Not at all! As soon as you let them loose, they would fly away—and worse still, they would bring wild partridges to eat your corn.

To debate the matter was useless. The white men, however,

had stronger arguments than words: the resistance of the chief began to melt before a roll of enticing red cloth. "How much of this will you give me?" he asked. But his interviewers demanded to see the child and were accordingly led to the lodge where he lay, tightly bound with thongs of rawhide, over which the contused flesh had swollen so that the strings could not be seen. The boy was almost starved and looked half dead, but began to revive after the visitors had, with difficulty, removed the thongs. They then offered ten yards of the red cloth in payment.

"Too little!" the chief grunted his refusal. His braves had had much trouble and danger in catching the prisoner and deserved a greater reward.

"That's all we'll give!" flared Sylvester, turning angrily to his followers. Were they then to be robbed by these red devils? No, they would take the child whether or not the ransom price was accepted!

A shout of approval greeted this rash proposal. And Sylvester's men snatched the child from the startled savages and recklessly carried it to their encampment, where all the whites were ordered to be ready with their guns. Thus a major outbreak seemed in the making. Though many of the whites would have slain an adult Indian with no more compunction than if he had been a squirrel, apparently none of them saw any inconsistency in risking their lives over a papoose.

In this crisis, when the air was tense with impending conflict and Pattie's fighters were already throwing up a barricade, the one man who seems to have kept his head was the Indian chief.

"So? You think you are strong enough to take the child by force?" he asked in incredulous surprise, as he stared Sylvester full in the face.

But Sylvester bullishly held to his point. They would keep the child—yes, they would keep it even if they all died in the effort. For then they would be avenged by their countrymen, who would come and slay their slayers.

Still imperturbable in the face of this melodramatic outburst, the Indian merely offered some advice. "Keep your powder and lead, palefaces, to kill buffaloes and your enemies!" He did not wish to arouse the enmity of their countrymen; besides, he had made a vow to kill no more white men. And so, if they would give him the cloth, plus a certain vermilion paper, he would let them have the child.

The deal was quickly completed, for the vermilion paper was a trinket, meant merely for trading with the Indians.

Under the care of the whites, the boy quickly recovered and soon became a general favorite as he played about the camp. But how, among this party of roving, unattached males, could he be provided for permanently? This question was to receive an unexpected answer.

One day they reached a small Indian camp, containing about thirty women and children in addition to some men. The little boy was romping as usual among the whites, when suddenly they heard loud cries and saw the child in the arms of an Indian, who hugged and kissed him demonstratively. From the man's gestures, they knew that he was the boy's father.

In reply to his subsequent speech, of which they understood not a syllable, they tried to explain how they had come into charge of the child. All that he could make out was one word, Pawnee—but this was enough. At this hated sound he rushed into his tent; dashed out again with his bow and arrows and two Indian scalps; made signs to indicate that he had obtained them during the fight when he lost the child; then placed them where he could shoot his arrows through them, as a proof of his contempt for all Pawnees. Finally, in order to show his gratitude, he made the elder Pattie a gift of a pipe and a pair of leggings, with porcupine-quill decorations, and bore his child with him into his tent for the night.

Next morning the Patties witnessed a ceremony. Just as the planet Venus glittered above the horizon, they heard a crying and a shouting and saw the Indians prostrating themselves, with their faces to the ground. In a little while they arose and ringed themselves about the fire, while they lighted a pipe and blew the smoke first toward the rising sun, then toward the zenith. By this means they wished to thank the Great Spirit for letting them see another day.

The trappers' next contacts with the Indians, not long after leaving the boy and his father, were less amicable. One evening, when rain had caused them to relax their caution, they were greeted by a shower of arrows from some natives whose names Jim gives as Arrockarees. In the resultant skirmish—doubtless a fearsome affair, with men shouting and screaming and the deadly missiles flying in all directions—two horses and four Indians were killed, while one Indian was gravely wounded and one white man slightly injured.

But this was a mere passing affray, recorded in matter-of-fact language in a single short paragraph of the Personal Narrative.

A few days later the travelers were involved in some more serious shooting. They came upon the bodies of two scalped men, so badly mutilated by wild animals that it was impossible to judge anything of their identity except that they had been whites. All about them arrows were sticking out of the ground, and nearby, on soil trampled by hoofs and feet, testimony to the ferocity of the battle was found in the shape of five dead Indians. The members of Pattie's party, as they buried the remains of their fellow whites, were not only horrified but infuriated. True, they knew nothing whatever of the cause of the fight, nor whether it had been due solely to the treachery of the Indians; the silence of the Personal Narrative on this point is eloquent, as is the fact that the author apparently saw no need to defend or explain his comrades' immediate demand for revenge.

A few miles upstream they saw signs of Indians and sent ten scouts ahead. After about four miles the party, which included Jim, made out about twenty Indian fires a few hundred yards away and debated whether to begin shooting. But for reasons of prudence they decided to return to camp and report what they had seen; and consequently sixty men, headed by Sylvester Pattie, set out with the idea of surrounding the Indians before dawn. Jim insisted upon joining them, since, as he said, he would not have liked his father to go into battle without him.

About midnight they approached the Indian camp, and three hours later they had posted themselves all about it, while the savages slept on. But the attackers were to hold their fire until Sylvester gave the word. In the revealing frankness of the *Personal Narrative* we have further insights into the attitude of mind of the men—an attitude reminding us of a hunter who gloatingly catches a stag in the sights of his rifle:

> As an Indian occasionally arose and stood for a moment before the fire, I involuntarily took aim, with the thought, how easily I could destroy him, but my orders withheld me.

Remember that the narrator is the same man who, only a short time before, had been infuriated at the killing of white men by the Indians.

All through the night the prowlers waited for their prey, and at dawn two of them were discovered by the Indians, who instantly raised the war cry and began to attack. Under Sylvester's order the whites fired back, and in an action lasting about fifteen minutes, they put the Indians to rout. Truly this was a battle, even if a small one. The casualties included

one white man mortally wounded, thirty Indians slain, and
ten taken prisoner.

The prisoners were at once put to work burying the dead
and subsequently were questioned and admitted having belonged to the party that had killed the white men; they
explained that the whites had been killed on the orders of
their chief because they had refused to share their powder
and balls. The futility of the entire undertaking was under-
scored by the fact that they had gained but little powder or
shot, but had lost four braves in the initial engagement, in
addition to the thirty shot down in the subsequent encounter.

And the white men—what had they gained? Presumably
they had earned some credit when they released the prisoners,
gave them back their bows and arrows, and warned them not
to kill any more white men. In freeing the captives the whites
showed themselves in some ways superior to the savages, who
often tortured prisoners of war to death. One of the warriors
seemed to recognize this in his own way when, upon regaining
his freedom, he gave Sylvester Pattie an eagle's feather, called
him good and brave, and said that he would never kill another
white man.

But in the long run what could vengeful attacks accomplish
except still further to inflame the relations between the races?
One does not have to look deeper for one of the root reasons
for the whole series of Indian wars that have ensanguined the
history of North America.

It was not long before the Patties had a fresh brush with
the Indians. The first indications of danger were borne to them
by large herds of buffaloes, all running in one direction,
parallel to the white men's course. During two successive days
the flight of the animals continued, as if something were
pursuing them; and on the evening of the second day the
travelers reached the main stream of the Arkansas, where
they hastened to pitch their tents and make their fires before

the threatening skies released the rain. As the smell of roasting meat came to their nostrils, they saw some Indians staring down at them from a ridge about half a mile away; and, knowing the ways of the redmen, they hurriedly tied their horses and mules.

But after a few minutes some of the savages approached, guns on shoulders, in an open way which did much to disarm suspicion. "Amigo! Amigo!" they called out, halting not far off, and one of the whites threw back the answer, "Amigo! Amigo!"

The Indians, who revealed themselves as Comanches, then drew up to the white party. Fortunately one of the whites understood their language and was able to act as interpreter.

"Who is your leader?" the chief asked boldly. Immediately he was introduced to Sylvester and told him that the whites should encamp among his people, since they were all good friends.

Sylvester, suspicious of such impromptu fellowship, replied that they had made camp before knowing where the Indians were, and could not move now for fear of ruining their goods in the rain.

However, the chief insisted that, now that the whites knew where his tribe was, they must move at once. But Sylvester, still doubting the intentions of the savages, replied that he would move next morning if it did not rain. And at this the chief threw out an ultimatum. Either the white men would come with him at once, or his braves would overwhelm and kill them and take everything they possessed!

Brusque words only bred brusque words. If the chief sent his men, Pattie promised, they would be shot down as fast as they arrived. And to emphasize his intentions, he shoved the Comanche out of his tent.

Immediately the Indian, pointing to the spot where the

sun would be at about eight in the morning, hurled a second ultimatum. Pattie's party must be at the camp by the indicated time! Otherwise, they must deal with his warriors!

As the Comanche left through the rain that was just beginning to fall, Pattie's men set to work, building a breastwork of logs and tying the mules and horses in a depression between the camp and the river, in the expectation of an attack before morning. But a sleepless night passed without any assault, and no sign of danger appeared until about eight o'clock, when an army of Comanches burst into view, armed with flintlock muskets, spears, and shields, and with black, painted faces hideously leering. The *Personal Narrative* gives their number as six or eight hundred, which sounds excessive, the more so as far fewer might have made an imposing display.

After a few shots had been fired at the approaching party, one of the Indians rushed at full speed toward the whites and threw down his bow and arrows. "Comanches no good, me Iotan!" he exclaimed in broken English; and went on to explain that the Iotan people were near at hand and would not let the Comanches hurt the whites.

The latter, not realizing that the Iotans were only a faction of the Comanche tribe, were impressed. And after about an hour, during which the Comanches discharged some shots at a safe distance, the onlookers were delighted to see a new armed band, apparently of Iotans, interposing themselves between the whites and the Comanches.

Now the conflict shifted to the Comanches and the Iotans, who began firing upon one another, while the air was shaken with their war yells and by the shrieks and howls of the wounded and dying. Gladly the Patties and their comrades would have thrown themselves in to aid the Iotans; but amid the close-packed ranks, they could not tell friend from foe. Then to their delight, after about a quarter of an hour, they saw that the Comanches were dismounted—the sign of their defeat.

The Iotans immediately left to get their women and children, and led them near the white camp, while the chief pitched his tent amid the white men. The wounded Iotans, ten in all—two of them mortally injured—were then brought up; and soon afterward the Comanche chief was summoned by the Iotan, and peace negotiations began. The terms were quickly agreed upon: for every Comanche warrior who had been killed beyond the number of slain Iotans, the Comanche chief would receive two horses. With this settlement, which was supplemented by the payment to the Iotans by the whites of goods worth a hundred dollars, the victorious chief professed himself well contented.

But to the Patties these arrangements seemed a little strange. Why was it that the winners had to pay an indemnity—and, still more surprising, appeared pleased to pay? The settlement, so queer by the white men's standards, was quite in harmony with the customs and psychology of the red men. Four years before, the father of the Iotan chief, who likewise had been a chief, had gone with the Comanches to hunt for buffaloes, and the Comanches, having joined forces with some Navahos, had treacherously slain the elder Iotan chief and most of his men. For this outrage the Comanches had paid a penalty of twenty horses for the father and four horses for every other warrior. But now the son, according to his way of thinking, had more than evened up the score, since he had given only two horses for every Comanche he had killed.

"I am happy," Jim reports him as saying. "I have killed three times as many of them, as they did of us, and paid less for it." Altogether a notable victory!

Sylvester, in thanking the Iotan, expressed regret for the

lost men. But the Indian, though acknowledging that they had been brave, did not look on matters of life and death in the dreary way of the whites. "They loved my father," he said, "whom they have gone to see, where they will have plenty to eat, and drink, without having to fight for it."

Still not giving up hope, the defeated Comanche chief now asked and received permission to speak with the whites. Gone was last evening's bravado; all that he wished, he asserted, was to make peace with the white men and obtain some powder and ball. To this the Patties, as might have been expected, replied with an emphatic "No!" But they, too, wished peace and would make an agreement with him if he promised never again to kill a white man.

The Indian, if one could believe his protests, had never killed nor intended to kill any white man. He had merely wanted to get ahead of the Iotans in the trading. However, with a trace of his old effrontery, he added that since he had been so disappointed in his dealings, he thought that he deserved a little powder and ball by way of compensation.

An abrupt "No!" was the response to this request also. But in return for a treaty of peace, the Patties agreed to give the chief a letter of recommendation to the next party of traders who came that way. We read in the *Personal Narrative* no estimate as to how much such a letter was likely to be worth.

Finally, becoming friendly, the chief asked the whites not to make war on him even if he should accidentally kill some of their men. Any such little mishap could easily be adjusted; he would do the honorable thing and pay for the victims with horses or beaver skins.

The white men, disgusted with this proposal, surely did not know that it was consistent with the customs and the ways of thinking of many uncivilized and half-civilized peoples, and was not far out of line with the *wertgilt*, or established scale of money payments for crime, which had existed among their own Teutonic ancestors. Callous as any such arrangement may seem, it represented a great step forward from the unrestricted blood feud, the only likely alternative.

3

Episodes among the Spaniards

IN LATE October the party reached San Fernando de Taos,
about seventy-five miles northeast of Santa Fe. And there
they had their first contacts with the Spaniards and found
them not at all as expected. The men, with their short red-
belted pantaloons and buckskin leggings, their long jackets
or serapes thrown over their shoulders, and the small swords
and knives at their sides, did not in the least look like the
Americans. And the women, with their red or blue belts, the
scarves about their shoulders, and their short petticoats, were
poorly appareled, but made up in hospitality for what they
lacked in appearance, and brought the strangers food and
invited them into their houses to eat.

As an example of their simple, friendly spirit, Jim mentions
that the first time he and his father were walking on the street,
they were greeted by a woman who was standing in a doorway
and who made signs for them to enter. Having led them up a
flight of steps to a neatly whitewashed room adorned with

36

images of saints and a brass crucifix, she treated them to wine and a dish of red pepper and corn (which they could not eat), along with some tortillas and milk. Despite the handicaps of language, they remained until evening, when the bells began to ring and she and her children went down on their knees in prayer.

A few days later they reached Santa Fe, which impressed them with its flat-roofed houses, its pleasant stream, its cultivated surrounding plain, its enticing views of far-off snow-clad mountains, and its numerous churches with their many bells, whose noise "would almost seem sufficient to waken the dead."

At Santa Fe they were plunged into another of their numerous adventures. At about ten in the night the whole town was awakened by the sound of the drum, the fife, and the French horn. Screams, shouts, and yells broke out; men and women began dashing wildly about, many of them drawn to the scene of the drumbeating in the public square. By the light of the moon the Patties could see a crowd rushing toward them, and, seizing their guns, they prepared to defend themselves. But the light was just sufficient for them to identify the seeming aggressors as harmless, excited women, who were shrieking something about the Comanches being in the town, massacring its inhabitants.

During the long remaining hours of the night the Patties, picturing the Indians as skulking about in the darkness and striking down helpless victims, fearfully awaited an attack. But no further incident came before dawn, when they received a visit from the governor, who told them that the women had the story wrong. No Comanches had attacked the town. Not that something serious enough had not happened! On the Rio Pacos, the present-day Pecos River, the large tributary of the Rio Grande which rises in the mountains east of Santa Fe, the Indians had burst into the ranches of some of the wealthy

Spaniards, and had robbed and murdered several families, and had made prisoners of five women: one American and four Spaniards, among them the daughter of the former governor.

"Will you help us recapture these women?" the present governor appealed to the Patties.

They agreed at once, made their preparations, and set out with four hundred mounted men.

For three days they rode on the trail of the Indians, until at last, one morning at about eight, they came in sight of the smoking fires of an abandoned native camp. But it was noon when, after pressing on at greater speed, they first saw the Comanches themselves moving toward a stream-threaded pass in the mountains. The Spanish commander now approached Sylvester with the request that he take charge of the entire enterprise, and swore that he and his troops would obey their new chief.

Sylvester, having been persuaded to accept, was not long in forming a plan. The Spaniards were ordered to follow the Indians, while keeping out of their sight; and Pattie's own party, hidden from view by the hills, would take a roundabout route in order to reach a place of concealment in front of the red men. Thus the enemy would be caught, as it were, between the jaws of pincers: the Spaniards would close in from the rear while Pattie and his men were firing in front; and the Indians, taken by surprise, would have no time to kill their prisoners.

To this scheme the Spaniards at once agreed; and Sylvester, having reached a hollow in the path of the Indians, stationed his men in a semicircle with their horses tied behind them, and ordered each man to prime and pick his gun afresh. The first object of attack was to be the Indians immediately around the captive women.

For an hour and a half the men waited before the tensely expected moment arrived. Then from behind their screen of trees and rocks they could hear the sound of a great host approaching. The first things that struck their eyes were sheep and horses in a large flock; and behind these animals, driving them forward, were the five captives, all stark naked, and with the Indians immediately in their rear.

Sylvester waited until the savages were within thirty or forty yards; then he ordered, "Fire!" As the shots rang out, the prisoners started at a run toward the white men. "Save the women!" cries rang out. "Save the women!" But already for three of the victims it was too late: transfixed by spears thrown from behind, they fell shrieking to earth. Jim and a companion meanwhile sprang forward to rescue the remaining two women, but the companion, too, was struck by an arrow. Meanwhile an Indian, his arm raised in the very act of attacking one of the surviving captives, was brought to earth by a bullet. And the two women, crying out in terror and relief, managed to reach Jim, who, aided by his comrades, hastily wrapped blankets about them in order to shield them from the cold. Jim had hardly time to notice that one of the rescued pair was Jacova, a beautiful black-eyed señorita, the daughter of the ex-governor. The battle, which still raged on, demanded all his attention.

Sylvester, as he pressed the Indians back, expected the Spaniards to close in from the rear according to plan, so as to catch the enemy between them. But no Spaniards were to be seen—not until the Indians had been driven back through the gap in the mountains, when, hearing the bloodcurdling yells of the savages, the four hundred allies fired a single volley and dashed away. Their horses were good, and the Indians did not try to intercept them; instead, they rushed back on Pattie and his men, who, being comparatively few, were forced to retreat and take shelter in the woods.

For about ten minutes a deadly conflict was waged at pistol point, while Sylvester directed his men to fire from

behind the trees, conserving every shot. The Indians, still
yelling like all the fiends of the Inferno, fought bravely, but
in the end they retreated once more; and the Spaniards joined
in the pursuit, though they still cautiously remained out of
gunshot. Ten men, however, had been lost from Pattie's
party, and one of Sylvester's shoulders was becoming stiff
and swollen from an arrow wound.

But now the Spaniards, though they had suffered no losses
and had contributed nothing to the defeat of the Comanches,
began strutting about in the joy of victory. With the same
butchering exultation manifested by warriors in many a greater
battle, they slew a wounded Indian and rode over the bodies
of the slain, thrusting their spears through them in order to
make an end of any who still preserved the breath of life.
But Sylvester ordered them to cease these brutalities or be
fired upon, and the Spanish leader added a similar command
and then asked Sylvester to deliver the two rescued women
over to him. And at this another feud broke out.

What right, Pattie wanted to know, had the Spaniards to
demand the women, when they had not had the courage to
join in rescuing them? This naturally enraged the officer, who
pleaded that he had been unable to rally his men, and irrele-
vantly declared that he would not consider the women any
safer with the Americans than with the Indians, as they were
not Christians. This retort prompted a further exchange of
insults, and finally Sylvester announced that he would leave
it up to the women to say whom they wished to accompany.
And the women, who had overheard the discussion, instantly
decided the point. They would go with those who had risked
their lives in saving them, said the black-eyed Jacova, and
would offer up hourly prayers for the salvation of these men.
The other woman concurred—which left the Spanish officer
no choice but to grumble and curse and to return to Santa Fe
without the ladies.

Jacova then asked to speak to her rescuer, upon whom her dark, enchanting face beamed with great kindliness and gratitude. One naturally supposes that, in the best style of romantic fiction, a love affair might have developed; but the young man does not let us know much of what he felt, though he does mention the girl's loveliness and adds that he was embarrassed at her compliments, as he saw no merit in what he had done, and regarded it merely as a duty performed.

Jacova, for her part, appears to have been at no pains to conceal her feelings, though at first they may not have extended beyond mere gratitude. After Jim had returned to Santa Fe and she saw that his clothes were soiled and stained by the dust and dirt of the journey, she brought him some others belonging to her brother-in-law, and when he at first refused them, she seemed so much hurt he felt obliged to accept. Then, showing him a leather hunting jacket that he had thrown over her upon rescuing her from the Indians, she swore that she would keep it as a memento as long as she lived.

On several occasions he was to have further contacts with the girl. Once, after he and his comrades had returned sick and ragged from the desert, she wept to see Jim reduced, as he puts it, "to skin and bone," his hair hanging "matted and uncombed," his head covered with an old straw hat, his clothing caked with dirt. Despite his wretched appearance, Jacova welcomed him as warmly as if he had been clad like an earl.

On a later meeting he was received by her with an "affectionate greeting." He had, besides, the benefit of her earnest advice: to discontinue his wandering life, with all its perils and uncertainties, and settle down in a house of his own. What else was in her thoughts may be conjectured without too much difficulty; but Jim, whether or not he was astute enough to read the feminine mind, gave no evidence of any romantic dreams when, after thanking her for her counsel, he promised to do as she recommended—after another year spent in the wilderness. It is not thus that a love-stricken man speaks.

And so in the end it was the roving life that dominated. On at least one other occasion he and Jacova were to meet; and this time she received him "with a partial embrace and a manner of constrained politeness," but showed great concern over a minor wound he had received. Then they had a long conversation on subjects not disclosed; and when they parted, they implored God to permit them to meet again.

This plea, however, was not to be granted. One imagines that Providence would have required a little more cooperation if these two were to be reunited. But for Jim, as for many another in the wild, alluring open spaces, the call of adventure was to prove stronger than the enticement of warm, twining arms and lustrous, bewitching dark eyes.

4

Encounters with Wild Animals

ONE OF the saddest facts about a vanished world is that it is
almost impossible to recreate it, even in imagination. Thus,
though little more than a century separates us from the virgin
prairies of the west, we seem almost as far from them as from
the dinosaur; and we can bring back the latter almost as
easily as the former. Today in the green fertile corn lands of
Iowa, the grain fields of Kansas and Nebraska, and the mil-
lions of acres of open range land farther west, we see nothing
to remind us of the abundant and varied wildlife familiar to
the pioneers. For this reason the pages of Pattie's book are
windows giving us glimpses, if only fleeting and partial
glimpses, into a universe that has faded forever.

Time after time the *Personal Narrative* makes casual reference to things that may have seemed commonplace to the
writer but that appear strange and even wondrous to us, in
view of the fact that the great herds of bison have been re-
placed by droves of cows, and the vast flocks of passenger

pigeons, trumpeter swans, and other flying glories have been supplanted by barnyard fowl. Two facts stand out in the *Personal Narrative*: the land's natural endowment with a profusion of wild things of many varieties, and the white man's attitude toward those wild things.

We have all read, of course, of the uncountable bison that once roamed the plains, but we tend to forget that the bison were far from the only animals whose unchained multitudes populated the prairies. One is a little startled at a statement like: "As far as the plain was visible in all directions, innumerable herds of wild horses, buffaloes, antelopes, deer, elk, and wolves, fed in their fierce and wild freedom." The horses, to be sure, had come only with the white man; but the other animals had been here for thousands of years, though in a few years they would be largely or entirely extirpated.

One of the animals described by Pattie is the mountain sheep, which he saw in "multitudes"—a surprising fact in view of the comparative rarity of this creature in later days. He declares that one of them which his party killed had horns so large that each one would hold a gallon of water. Another animal that he depicts is the "wild hog"—by which he evidently means the peccary, which abounded in the American southwest and which, he truly states, was not at all like our domestic swine. He reports that it had no fear of man and was so ferocious that he was often compelled to climb a tree in order to escape its charge; and he adds that "we killed a great many, but could never bring ourselves to eat them."

In this remark one may read perhaps more than he intended to say, for he does not allege that the animals were killed chiefly out of self-defense. We get the same impression in many other instances, as when Pattie mentions that he got "the merriest sport imaginable" in chasing and shooting buffaloes, and when he tells how within two days, while camping near a hill of salt, he killed fifteen deer that came to lick salt. There is no suggestion that this many deer could have been used as food or for any other purpose by the comparatively small company. In no case do we find any appreciation of the animals as things worthy of existing for their own sakes, as things of joy, feeling, or beauty, as things forming a picturesque part of the natural background and having a place in the economy and balance of nature, or as things serving any possible purpose aside from the needs or pleasures of man. Not that the Patties were any more callous or shortsighted than other wanderers and adventurers; their attitude was merely typical of most.

The following statement is revealing: "Our companion, the old governor, was much amused, seeing us kill wild geese and prairie wolves with our rifles, the latter being abundant in this country." Prairie wolves, or coyotes, were of course of no value for food or for any other need of the hunters.

But while these animals and many others were slaughtered for no apparent reason, many were shot for their flesh, and large numbers were killed for their skins. And this was particularly true of the beavers, which were considered of great value for their fur and were the chief objects of some of the expeditions. How numerous these creatures were, and how they were hunted, is revealed in some of Pattie's reports.

For example, on their first night on the "Helay," or Gila, River of New Mexico they caught thirty beavers. A little later on a branch of the Gila, the San Francisco, they took no less than thirty-seven in one night. The total catch, in a few days' trapping, was two hundred and fifty animals. Not long afterward, on another tributary of the Gila to which they gave the name of Beaver River, they gathered another two hundred skins and only ceased the slaughter when their pack animals had all the furs they could carry. Subsequently, on the Colorado River, they had a similar success: one night they set forty traps and in the morning were elated to find thirty-six victims;

while on another night they reported exactly the same number, and on later occasions the morning take was as high as sixty beavers.

Little did they realize that, on many of the streams where this valuable animal was so abundant, beavers were soon to become extinct.

They might, however, have taken warning from their own observations—had they wished to take warning. Consider Pattie's statement about the country near the headwaters of the Yellowstone: "All these streams had been so much trapped as to yield but few beavers." And note this report on a stream in New Mexico: "We set our traps, but to no purpose, for the beavers were all caught, or alarmed."

And this was while the Far West was still largely an untrodden wilderness!

One of the most imposing beasts seen by the Patties is now extinct or virtually so in all of the United States south of Alaska. Wandering through the safe and secure farmlands, ranches, and ranges of the west, we would be astonished and terrified today to come upon the huge, lumbering grizzly bear, perhaps rearing itself to a seven-foot height while drawing wide its huge, hooked claws. Yet in the prairies, as among the mountains, this creature was once at home. In a single day's travel in what are now the plains of western Kansas, not far from the Colorado border, Pattie counted two hundred and twenty of these animals, which he calls "white bears." Considering that today in this region the nearest things in size to the grizzlies are our domestic cattle, this statement may appear incredible; but when we remember how many other wild animals the virgin plains supported, there is no reason to doubt Pattie's report.

Because of its great size and strength and because it had had no enemy to fear before the white man's arrival (except perhaps for Indians with their arrows), the grizzly was bold as well as redoubtable and would not hesitate to molest even man. Pattie tells us that, on the day on which the two hundred and twenty were counted, they killed eight which attacked them. Sometimes, however, the attack may have been provoked by the men, as in the case of the first grizzly Jim ever saw, which kept them busy for at least an hour, since "It was constantly in chase of one or another of us, thus withholding us from shooting at it, for fear of wounding each other."

Two days later, the report goes on, they "killed three white bears"—but we read no suggestion that the animals were the aggressors. And that very night a disaster occurred when a grizzly got in among the horses and seized one of them, while the others burst away in a stampede. The bear, in the act of devouring the still living horse, was wounded by a shot from Jim's rifle—which only served to infuriate the predator, causing it to growl and to tear up the ground all about it with its powerful claws. Amid the darkness and confusion some of the men came too near the enraged beast, and it charged, catching one, who screamed in agony. A second shot put an end to it, but the shot had come too late. The caught man had been mangled so badly that it seemed unlikely he would live; and after a three days' wait he was left behind with two comrades, who would care for him as long as he remained alive.

Nor was this the only case in which the bears wreaked havoc, both on domestic animals and on man. We are told how in some districts, when the farmers heard a noise in their corn fields and got up in the night in the belief that the commotion had been caused by cows or horses that had broken into their land, they might find themselves confronted by grizzlies, possibly with fatal results. Jim mentions a case in New Mexico, in which he himself was involved. A servant of his named Iago went with another man for a load of wood, when suddenly they came upon a bear, who killed Iago and also a donkey in his team. We are left to guess whether the grizzly first attacked the donkey, and slew the man when he came to the defense of the beast, though this sequence of events is not improbable; but we are informed that Jim and a number of companions, including some Spaniards, went out to kill the bear, trailed it to its den in a crevice in the bluff, and slew it when it approached them in defiant fierceness.

Whether or not the bear in this case made the first attack, in other cases the men were the aggressors. One such episode occurred after a night of storm and snow, when the horses in their impatience had broken away and Jim and a companion had set out in search of them. While following the trail of the animals, they passed a cave at the foot of some cliffs and found the bushes beaten down, as though some monster had been browsing near. Believing that a bear was inside the cave, the men collected some pine knots, which they split with their tomahawks and used as torches. Jim then invited his comrade to accompany him inside the cave, so that they might shoot the bear, but the other man, not craving close contact with a grizzly, refused the invitation in no undecided terms. Jim pleaded, however, that he had more than once joined his friend in similar attacks; and besides, he pointed out, a bear in its den was less to be feared than one in the woods. But these arguments did not impress his comrade.

Jim therefore decided on a one-man grizzly hunt. Daringly he entered the cave, guided by the light of his torch, which he had lashed to a stick in a way to parallel his gun barrel. For about twenty paces he moved forward cautiously, but saw nothing. Then, no more than about seven feet ahead, he heard a growl and a gnashing of teeth, and the beast lunged up to its full height in front of him. Instantly he fired between the creature's eyes, turned, and raced away. But he was in too great a hurry. He stumbled, and his light went out. Again he shot to his feet, and again in his haste he fell. This mishap was repeated several times, while he cut his limbs on the sharp rocks and lost his gun. From the dread darkness behind him he could hear the bear growling and struggling, and imagined it to be just at his heels.

But somehow he reached the light again—reached it, his comrade remarked, "as pale as a corpse." However, the episode was not yet over; he must go back into the cave in order to retrieve his gun. A considerable time passed before he could steel himself to the effort; and then, having borrowed his companion's rifle, he entered in greater terror than he may have been willing to admit. Pausing and listening, he advanced slowly; to his relief, all was silent. After a little while, he came upon his gun and was rejoiced to find the bear—killed by his single shot.

This grizzly was, he adds, the largest he ever saw; the two men extracted ten gallons of oil from its carcass and cached this booty in a crevice of the cliff, along with the meat, which they dried. But though these provisions turned out to be highly useful, Jim's father reprimanded him severely when he heard of the exploit: if the first shot had failed to take effect, Sylvester pointed out, no power on earth could have saved him from the jaws of the infuriated beast.

One cannot help suspecting that, had the youth paid with his life for his unprovoked and foolhardy attack, the story would have been spread abroad of one more bloodthirsty assault by a bear.

In other cases also the really murderous beast is not the bear. We observe this in a later instance, in which Jim has gone hunting with a companion (whose name is not given, though we are told that he was an American). The companion had killed a deer on a high ridge and had carelessly started skinning it before reloading his rifle. In his preoccupation, he did not see a bear and her three cubs, which, doubtless, attracted by the odor of the meat, had approached to within a few feet of him. The startled men did not wait to argue over the prey;

abandoning the deer, they rushed away in terror of death. The beasts, however, being more interested in the venison than in the men, proceeded to have dinner.

But Jim and his companion could not leave the mother un-molested. After a time they started back toward the ridge, in order to have, as he puts it, "the sport of hunting the animal." As they approached the ridge, they saw the enemy descending toward them, and at once took places behind trees and rocks, from which to shoot the unwary prey. But the first shot only wounded the enemy, which ran at Jim's companion in a fury and chased him up a tree. Finding itself unable, after some efforts, to tear down the tree, it rushed toward Jim, growling and clawing up the bushes as it came. Jim aimed at the crea-ture's head, but waited till it was within six feet, when unfor-tunately his gun misfired. Then, still growling, and with mouth wide open, the bear sprang at him.

In the terror of that instant, in his frenzy to get away, he fell—fell over a precipice he had not noticed before, splitting his jawbone on a sharp rock and knocking himself insensible. When he regained consciousness after perhaps an hour, his companion was sitting over him with a hat full of water, bleed-ing him with a butcher knife—as if he had not already bled sufficiently from the wound in his chin!

One might suppose that this would have ended the bear hunt. But no! A mere broken chin must not impede so im-portant a project. Jim's ardor, it is true, had considerably cooled; he was willing to quit the adventure. But the other man insisted that they go on, and, regardless of his wounds, Jim finally consented. After climbing some trees and making a noise to attract the bear's attention, they dispatched the animal. But they were less successful with the three cubs, though these, which were about as big as large raccoons, were soon overtaken by Jim's companion, who dashed after them afoot. One reads without much regret that "These imps of the devil turned upon him and made him fight"—in fact, turned upon him so savagely that it was all he could do to get away, retreating ingloriously with a pair of deeply bitten and scratched legs.

Whether the cubs were able to survive without their mother is another question.

5

Over Mountain and Desert

THE MOST striking adventures of the Patties began only after they had reached Santa Fe. Being much too large and cumbrous, Pratte's company of more than a hundred had been split into small bands. The group to which the Patties belonged consisted of no more than seven men and, after receiving a trapping license, set out along the Gila River, which Jim supposed to be unexplored, though in fact it had been known ever since the coming of the first white men. Within a short time their company was doubled by the addition of seven hunters who were traveling in their direction and would help to guard them against the hostile Indians with whom the country was thought to bristle.

After a few days and a stop at the Santa Rita de Cobra copper mines in present-day Grant County, they came to a canyoned country perhaps of great beauty but also of unusual difficulty. At one point Jim and a companion, leaving the main company, followed a clear, fish-filled stream about thirty yards wide, but had to scramble beneath the cliffs on ledges so narrow that they sometimes were forced down on hands and knees amid the dense brush, and were compelled to cross the river thirty-six times in one day (presumably by fording it). Worse still, perhaps, was the danger of coming face to face with a grizzly at any turn. But this was one of the ordinary hazards of the wilderness.

They dared still greater hazards when Jim and his companion, reaching a fork in the river, agreed to separate, so that each might explore one of the branches of the river. Jim, as he proceeded alone through a very brushy region, was not only cautious but fearful, as he had never before been in the woods all by himself and the country abounded in bears. That night he camped near a pile of driftwood, of which he made a fire, so as to frighten off any roving predators; then he placed a spit with a turkey before the flames to roast. After eating, he lay down beside a log, with his gun at his right hand . . . but it was long before he slept. Doubtless the night noises—the whirring of insects, the threshing and murmuring of the river, the cracking of twigs where some unseen creature passed, the hoots and faint cries of distant wood dwellers, the remote scream of some caught animal—all forced themselves upon his consciousness. How well he must have known, as every woodsman knows, that the wilderness at night is not silent!

Finally his weariness asserted itself. It may have been much later when abruptly he awakened. What was that faint stirring among the leaves? Cautiously he raised his head; there, in the dim light, he saw a long cat form stretched out on the log under which he was lying.

With the careful aim of one who knows that a false move will mean death, Jim raised his rifle and fired at the puma's head. Then, not knowing that his first shot had killed the animal, he sprang to his feet, dashed back about ten yards, and hastily reloaded his rifle.

He was in the act of reloading when he heard a shot from the other fork of the river, which was separated from his own branch only by a narrow ridge. A second shot followed almost immediately, making him fear that his comrade had been attacked by Indians.

Without delay, therefore, he set out toward the junction of the rivers, though he does not say how he managed this difficult feat by night. One must assume that he had bright moonlight to guide him. In any case he tells us that he reached his destination by dawn, and found his comrade quite whole and unmolested by Indians. The other man, awakened by Jim's shot, had seen a bear standing on its hind legs, growling at him, only a few yards away; and had fired at it first with his rifle, then with his pistol, though with what results we are not informed. At the very moment when Jim had supposed him to be under Indian attack, he had imagined that the savages were assaulting Jim.

Soon afterward the two men rejoined the main party, which for a time was doomed to bitter privations, since the country had already been so stripped of wildlife that they could find almost nothing to eat. During an entire period of four days the travelers, once more numbering seven, had no food at all except one hare caught by one of their dogs; they became so weak that they were forced reluctantly to kill a horse in order to remain alive.

A few days later, in early January 1825, their strength and their spirits were restored by a catch of thirty-seven beavers, and they pushed on with fresh energy, though the period of relative ease and plenty was to be no more than an interlude. The graph of their travels might be described as a series of steep ascents and dips, in which they were alternately rising to altitudes of exhilaration and hope and slipping back into gulfs of hardship and despair.

Sometime later they reached a pass in the mountains, from

which, as the *Personal Narrative* describes it, "On every side the peaks of ragged and frowning mountains rose above the clouds, affording a prospect of dreariness and desolation, to chill the heart." To the traveler of a later day, riding in cushioned ease in a private car along those same mountains or soaring above them at nine or ten miles a minute in a jet plane, the ranges may present panoramas of startling and inspiring beauty. But not so to the Patties, who trailed, poorly clad, across heights so cold that they had to keep active merely in order to avoid freezing. Even when, to their delight, they found a way to descend, their hardships were far from over, and their minds were fixed on anything but the grandeur of the scene. Time after time, as they wound down through a canyon, where a stream foamed so far below them that they could hardly see the waters, they were forced to unload the mules and horses and to carry the baggage by hand from precipice to precipice. Meanwhile the animals were constantly losing their foothold, were bruising and straining their limbs, and eventually were so exhausted that they could go no farther, and obliged the party to halt for two days. Worst still, the men, after a week of trudging through the mountains, had used all their provisions!

Seeking a way out of the perilous impasse, Jim and a companion named Allen climbed the highest peak in the vicinity, from which they could trace the course of the river in several places. Strangely, they were actually pleased to see the smoke rising from several Indian camps! Amid the vast, unhuman desolation, as Jim later reported, "To meet even enemies, was more tolerable, than thus miserably to perish with hunger and cold in the mountains."

Then painfully the party resumed its journey, and after three days, though we are not told how they kept up life in the interval, they reached the banks of the river. And there they did find food, "a little mush prepared from the seeds of grass," which some Indians had left behind as they fled in a panic at the approach of the whites, and which the starving whites devoured ravenously.

Now occurred various encounters with the Indians—encounters in which the intruders did not always emerge with first honors. They suffered their worst loss one day when the Indians stole all their horses and mules; without these creatures they were about in the position of a motor caravan stranded in the heart of the desert with no gasoline or gasoline stations, and no hope of relief from passing travelers. They did retrieve the loss to some extent by seizing four of the Indians' horses, but these were not enough. After all the trials and terrors they had endured in order to obtain the beaver furs, the main object of their expedition had been frustrated; they no longer had any way to transport the furs, and had no choice except to bury them in the hope of recovering them later. At a point which they knew at Battle-hill on the Beaver River, they packed their four horses with the remaining provisions and two traps and set out on the return trip, though not without fear of the Indians, which forced them to keep a strict watch at night and to do without a fire.

But this was not their worst privation. During the trek back over the dread mountain pass, the party had nothing to eat but the flesh of two beavers, whose skins they had prepared to serve as water bags. Meanwhile, his age telling upon him in the competition with much younger men, Sylvester grew weak and faint beneath the stress of the climb. For two days the men had neither food nor drink; but after descending to the plains, Jim killed an antelope, whose warm blood they drank, and found to be "refreshing, tasting like fresh milk." Water now was more of a problem than food; after a whole day's march, during which they pushed with parched lips and throats across a barren plain, all that they could find was a little moisture in the basin of a rock—barely enough for the men, with not a drop for any of the four horses, which shared their thirst and whose feet were bleeding from the rocks of the wilderness. The narrator strikes a sympathetic note by expressing his feelings for the horses, and even more for the dogs:

It went still more to my heart, to see my two faithful dogs, which had followed me all the way from my father's house, where there was always *bread enough and to spare*, looking at me with an expression, which a hunter only in the desert can understand, as though begging for food and water.

But worse was to follow. Sometime later, after being reduced to cooking the unsavory flesh of a buzzard, the men turned for food to the dogs themselves. Sylvester drew lots, to determine who should kill one of the animals, but Jim refused to participate, for fear that the unlucky chance would fall on him. The dogs, he says, were so dear to him that he would not have killed one of them in order to save his own life, but when the life of his father was at stake, he could not protest.

In any event, the expedition did, by whatever means, eventually make its way back to the copper mines, richer in nothing except grim and harrowing experiences and a cache of furs buried far away in the desert—furs that, in many a get-rich-quick vision, they dreamed of soon retrieving.

After reaching the copper mines, therefore, the Patties made plans to regain the furs. And as soon as possible Jim set out with fourteen companions and, after more than two weeks of travel, reached Battle-hill on the Beaver River. "I need not attempt to describe my feelings," he remarks, "for no description could paint them, when I found the furs all gone, and perceived that the Indians had discovered them and taken them away." Thus died his dream of wealth and prosperity! Now, even more ironically than when they had buried the furs, the adventurers were faced with the blank image of futility—a leering, mocking futility that had drawn them on through many burdensome days, alluring them over freezing mountains and burning deserts, causing them to shoot and to set traps and to decimate the country's animal life, while encouraged by golden pictures that were shown to have no more substance than a mirage.

True, this was but the common lot of most wanderers in unmapped lands. True, Jim did try to persuade himself (though doubtless without much success) "that repining was of no use." And in any case the situation of the Patties was far from hopeless: their immediate needs were cared for, and they were approached at the mines by the owner, Juan Unis, with a request that they stay with him for several months in order to protect the workmen from the Indians. And this offer they were glad to accept, though they were so grateful to Unis for his various kindnesses that they refused the proffered wages of a dollar a day. In that simple world of the backwoods, in which few things had to be bought and in fact few things could be bought, the Patties had little need for wages.

Thenceforth for a considerable time they employed themselves "most pleasantly in hunting deer and bears, of which there were great numbers in the vicinity." Jim also profited from the interval to learn Spanish from Juan Unis. But once more his old impatience at a settled life surged up within him; once more, despite all that he had suffered, he was drawn by the call of far horizons and unknown trails.

In September the Patties left on another trapping expedition, which occupied them until December, when they returned to the mines, where Sylvester received a tempting offer: Unis would rent the mines to him for five years at a thousand dollars a year and would furnish the first year's provisions as part of the agreement and pay Pattie for any improvements he might make. Such a generous proposal was not to be resisted, and the papers were soon drawn up.

For Jim, however, the tame, unadventurous life of a copper

miner had no charms. As if he had never done any traveling
at all, he was moved by the desire to see more of the country.
And so, heedless of the protests of his father, who graphically
pointed out the perils of the journey, he joined a company of
French trappers bound for the Red, or Colorado River.

Before very long he would learn how good a prophet
Sylvester had been. Yet the worst of the dangers might have
been avoided with a little prudence.

One evening the travelers reached a village of the Papawar
Indians, and the savages rushed forth to greet them with
painted faces and with bows and arrows, which alarmed the
white men, though the Indians threw down their weapons
when the whites assured them that they were friends. The
trappers now entered the village, and the Frenchmen began
strolling about curiously. Jim meanwhile was disturbed to see
several small knots of Indians talking earnestly among themselves; and he reported his observations to the French commander (whose name he does not give) and expressed the
fear that the Indians were plotting to hack them to bits. But
the Frenchman only laughed. *"Lâche! Poltron!"* he derided,
apparently regarding Jim as a coward and considering his
alarm childish. Jim, however, argued that caution was not
cowardice; but this only angered the Frenchman, who in
effect told his adviser to mind his own business.

Jim then whispered his suspicions to another Frenchman,
whom he had known from Missouri days; and he and this
man camped by themselves about a quarter of a mile from the
village. Just before sunset they saw their leader approaching
amid a crowd of Indians; and this only increased the fears
of Jim and his companion, who stated that the captain was so
sure of his own infallibility that he would take no one's advice.
The French captain then camped within about a hundred
yards of Pattie; and the Indians—several scores of them—were
demonstrative in helping him unload his mules. There would

be no harm, they assured him, in turning the animals loose: they, the Papawars, would see that they were well guarded. Certainly if the French leader supposed that the Indians could safely be put in charge of such valuable property as horses and mules, he was a man of a singularly trustful disposition. But he was doubly, triply, ten times more trustful if, as Jim claims, he consented to another proposal of the red men: to permit his arms to be stacked against a tree and even tied to the tree with ropes.

No wonder that Jim, resuming his argument with the captain, protested that this was a reckless act, that it was not necessary to show one's friendliness to the Indians by dispensing with all means of self-defense. But Jim might have known that he would be wasting his words. The Frenchman, more infuriated than ever, cursed him and repeated that he was a coward; and Jim retorted with various unflattering epithets, the least of which were "liar" and "fool." None of this, of course, could help anyone, except possibly the Indians.

But the Frenchman continued to mutter and swear while Jim returned to his own camp for supper. He had just eaten when he had the honor of a visit from the Indian chief, who tried to induce him and his companion to dine at the native camp, where they might enjoy some fine pumpkins, which had just been cooked for the white people. However, not even the love of pumpkins could entice Jim and his friend.

After a time, persuasion being ineffective, the chief turned to abuse and then to cajolery. The nights were cold, he said, and his braves were too poor to buy blankets; therefore he would like them to come and sleep with the whites, who had plenty of blankets. But this plea likewise failed to convince Jim. And so the chief tried his last argument: he was at war with another tribe of Indians, who might kill the whites in the night unless they came where he could protect them. But still Pattie refused to be protected.

After the chief had angrily left, Jim had another visitor: the French leader, who was more composed now, though he denounced his refractory follower for not coming to the Indian camp and so helping to placate the red men. But all that this visit produced was another exchange of insults.

As soon as the Frenchman had left, Jim and his companion, still persuaded that mischief was afoot, began to cut grass for their horses. But they did not unsaddle the animals, and they packed the mules, so as to be ready for instant flight. More important still, they remained awake.

Hours went by without incident. Then toward midnight a savage whistling shrilled forth, followed immediately by wild pandemonium: shrieks and groans, the crashing of clubs, the whoops of triumphant warriors. Amid the commotion Jim saw a shadowy group making toward him, and fired—which caused the shadows to retreat. But there was nothing they could do to help the Frenchmen, who, it was evident, were being massacred. It was all they could do to save themselves by mounting their horses and dashing off at the utmost speed possible in the darkness. As they rushed away, a single gunshot rang out from the Indian camp.

All night they pressed on toward a high mountain to the south; and when they reached it at dawn, they pushed their way about three miles up a creek that wound down a canyon. Here they halted for a time, for surely the Indians would not follow this far. While the animals were being fed, Jim's comrade passed about an hour on a climb to a high ridge, which would give him a bird's-eye view of the country. Upon his return he reported having seen something approaching along the plain. Jim, having hastily ascended the ridge, also saw the object—something vague and black, which after a time climbed a tree, leading the watchers to assume that it was a bear in quest of food.

Meanwhile far in the dim distance they could see smoke

rising from the Indian village. There doubtless the braves were even now dancing in high merriment about the scalps of the treacherously slain Frenchmen.

While the fugitives still watched, the supposed bear came down from the tree and drew near the creek on which they were encamped. Then they saw a glitter on its breast. The glitter of buttons! It was not a bear at all, but an Indian who had donned the coat of a murdered Frenchman!

Such was the watchers' not unnatural conclusion. But the savage was still far beyond rifle range. And when he had drawn closer, the men resolved to hold their fire until they were absolutely sure. And it was fortunate that they waited, for the man's skin did not show the expected dusky tint. After a time, in fact, they recognized him—the leader of the unfortunate French company!

The recognition had been mutual. Crying out with joy to see two fellow whites, the approaching man sank down in a faint. Exhausted, parched by thirst, and suffering from many deep wounds in his head and face, he was in a pitiable condition. However, after being given food and drink and having his wounds treated with some salve, he revived rapidly.

It is not surprising that in bitter remorse he bewailed his refusal to listen to Jim's advice. He then went on to tell of the Indian attack and of his escape owing to a pistol that he had kept in his pocket after all the other arms were stacked. A shot from the pistol had slain an assailant and enabled him to break away, though not before being wounded in several places by war clubs. As for his comrades—apparently he said little about them; there was little that could be said.

Toward dusk the watchers on the mountain made out three fires on the river bottom five miles away. These, they supposed, had been kindled by the Indians, who had set out in pursuit of the escaped men; for the savages, says Jim, were like some white people in that they "never forgive any persons that they have outraged or injured." What, therefore, should the three fugitives do? It was decided that the French captain should remain in charge of the horses while the other two went down to reconnoiter and try to discover how many Indians there were and whether it would be possible to steal past them.

When the two spies warily drew near the fires, they saw a large number of horses tied, with only two men to guard them. They crept to within fifty yards of the camp, but still could see only the two sentinels. Doubtless all the rest of the company were asleep somewhere out of sight. But before long surely some of them would rise, and then, as they passed between the white men and the fire, they would make easy targets.

At this point one or two questions assail the reader of the *Personal Narrative*. Since Pattie's professed purpose was to reconnoiter and try to discover how many Indians there were and whether it was possible to pass them, why should he want to kill the sentries? How could such bloodshed possibly further either of his announced objects? Would not the noise of the shots, on the contrary, arouse the Indians and consequently imperil him and his comrade and threaten their aims? One can understand the spirit of vengeance that filled him after the slaughter of the white men—the same murder lust that kindles a clansman in a blood feud. But could he be sure that the Indians in the camp were the Papawars who had perpetrated the outrage against the Frenchmen? Or was it merely that Indians, all Indians, were fair game, like grizzly bears and mountain lions, and might be shot whenever and whereever found?

In any event, it was well that the two scouts held their fire. They were near enough to hear a phrase from the lips of one of the sentries—near enough to hear him say in English, "Time to wake the relief guards!"

At this Jim sprang up and rushed incautiously toward the men. But his rashness nearly cost him his life. Startled at the apparition leaping up so strangely in the night, the sentries would have shot him had he not cried out, "A friend! A friend!"

Where in God's name had he come from? they demanded. But it did not take Jim long to explain who he was and what had happened; and soon the entire company were aroused and were listening to his story. There were twenty-nine men in the party, which was led by an American; and they at once agreed to join Jim in seeking vengeance against the Papawars.

Having fired twelve guns as a signal for the wounded Frenchman, who promptly came down from the mountain, the combined company proceeded to give a new demonstration of the ancient principle that violence breeds violence. With twenty men marching in front of the pack horses and twelve behind, they advanced toward the Indian village, making no fires on the way. Stealing along the dry old bed of a river, where they would be hidden by the high banks, they approached the village unobserved. The leader then ordered two of the men to show themselves above the bank; and these, as had been expected, were at once seen by the Indians, about two hundred of whom rushed toward them in a yelling mob, perhaps believing them to be Frenchmen who had escaped the massacre. Instantly the white men dropped out of sight and the Indians fanned out so as to catch them in a net, but did not suspect that this was bringing them close to the ambushed avengers.

When they were within about twenty yards, they were startled by a volley of shots; and while their assailants raked them with lead, they rushed off panic-stricken, men, women, and children racing toward a mountain less than half a mile away. Within a few minutes the village was deserted, except for one aged man who, being both deaf and blind, sat eating a sort of mush as placidly as if nothing had happened.

Leaving this poor old dodderer unmolested, the invaders proceeded to exercise the immemorial right of the victor to loot and despoil, and were not content until they had stripped the village of everything of value and set fire to the wigwams. A hundred and ten natives, Jim reports, probably with considerable exaggeration, had been slain, but he does not say whether women and children were among the victims. However, when shots are fired almost at random, how can all the women and children escape?

The red men having been taught the civilizing methods of the whites, the victors went on to take the Frenchmen's stolen horses and to bury the victims of the Indians' treachery, who had been horribly hacked to pieces. They then went on their way, ready for fresh adventures.

And fresh adventures awaited them in abundance. After various Indian episodes, which will be described in the next chapter, they reached one of the most scenic regions of the North American continent, the Grand Canyon of the Colorado; according to Pattie, it had never been explored, at least by Americans. Traveling through this whole magnificent region on the southern rim of the canyon, they were impressed by nothing so much as by the woeful difficulty of the journey. The snow lay on the ground to a depth of from twelve to eighteen inches; the river, thousands of feet below, twisted inaccessibly through its fantastic gulf; and the men, ill clad and near the end of their provisions, were shivering in the cold, while their horses could find little herbage and kept alive mainly on the bark of shrubs. Instead of the wonder and awe so frequently uttered by latter-day tourists, Jim has only a lament as to "these horrid mountains," and bewails that "A march more gloomy and heart-wearing . . . cannot be imagined." How astonished he would have been to learn that this desolate region was one day to be considered among the majesties of the land, one of the world's wonder spots!

With great relief the party eventually emerged from the canyon; renewed their supplies and their spirits by killing many beavers and elk; had a brush with a band of Indians, who attacked them and four of whom they killed; and kept on across vast distances to the Yellowstone and over the Great Divide, then through the land of the Blackfoots, then back to New Mexico and then down into the province of Sonora and even as far west as the waters of the Gulf of California. Only after many months did Jim return to the copper mines.

There he found his father in good health, but Sylvester was displeased with his son's long absence and exacted a promise from him to rove no more. And so for a time he remained with his parent and amused himself by hunting and by working in the gold mine. It was hardly likely, however, that a congenital wanderer of his type could be long tied down at any one place. But he could not have known that some of his most strenuous adventures lay ahead.

It was Sylvester himself who launched him into a lesser, though not unexciting, expedition in order to purchase some wine and whisky at Alopaz; at the mines these items sold for a dollar and a half a pint—in those days, a small fortune. Aided by a single Spanish servant and six pack mules, each of which had small barrels fastened over the saddles, Jim reached his destination, made his purchases, and, after some delay due to bad weather, started on the return trip. But with the return his troubles began.

The first difficulties were caused by the state of the roads, which a recent spring thaw had turned into quagmires, with the result that one of the mules gave out. Consequently the servant packed the load of the exhausted beast upon his riding animal, and had to walk. Passing through a wood, they saw some bear tracks, and the servant warned, "Have your gun ready!" But Jim, to his consternation, found that he had only one ball left and no means of making more. Here, surely, was a predicament! In a wild country where they might be attacked by the redoubtable grizzly if not by less powerful beasts or by hostile red men, a man without ammunition was about in the condition of a boxer with his arms tied. But of what use to reproach himself for his carelessness? He could only press on and pray to heaven to protect him. Meanwhile he would do his best to keep the facts from his servant, who would have turned back in terror had he known the truth, leaving Jim to complete the journey all by himself.

We can believe Jim's statement that he "advanced cautiously." We can also believe that he "passed a most uncomfortable night" out of fear of the bears which were just emerging from their hibernation with appetites well sharpened. "We and our mules," he reflects, "would have furnished them a delicious feast, after their hunger of months."

But apparently there were no bears at hand to take advantage of this rare opportunity. And on the following day fate smiled more brightly upon Jim.

In mid-morning he and his servant met a mounted Spaniard, who directed them to a party of friendly Apaches encamped near by, from whom Jim hoped to be able to buy a horse, so that the servant might once more ride. But the Spaniard, at the servant's suggestion and in return for a blanket, agreed to help them out of their difficulties by giving up his own horse. Evidently the purchasers did not pause to ask why the seller should part with the animal for so slight a consideration. The Apaches, however, were to enlighten them.

The two men did their best to pass the Indians unseen, but were betrayed by Jim's great straw hat, which reflected the sun when he lay down to rest. As Jim slept, four Indians rode up, and one of them hurled a spear at his neck, missing him by inches and pinning his hat to the ground.

Awakened thus rudely, he seized the spear to throw it at his attacker, who sprang out of range. He then rushed for his gun, which lay a few yards away, and aimed it at the Indian, but held his fire when to his astonishment the man called out, "Jim! Jim! Don't you know Targuarcha?"

The name was familiar. All at once Jim remembered an Indian who had belonged to a party at the mines and who had developed a slavish attachment to him. But why had Targuarcha tried to take his life?

The other Indians, gathering about and pointing at the servant's horse, quickly explained. The animal had been stolen from the Indians, and Targuarcha, not recognizing Jim beneath his big straw hat and taking him to be the thief, had sought vengeance. But now he earnestly begged Jim's pardon. And Jim, though convinced that Targuarcha really had not known who he was, nevertheless expressed his anger and his doubts of Targuarcha's good intentions. At this the Indian unbared his breast and cried out in Spanish, "If you think me such a traitor, kill me!"

This theatrical gesture was not without its effect. Jim and his would-be slayer were reconciled, while the Indians, to prove their good will, insisted on giving Jim the horse as a gift. At first he refused, and consented only after they had promised to accompany him back to the mines, along with their wives and children. Then after the servant had caused general laughter by crawling out from under the bushes, into which he had rushed for safety, they all set out amicably together.

Several days later they met the Apache chief, who agreed to join the company. And now Jim received another surprise. Almost within the hour, Jim saw Targuarcha approaching the chief with bare back, and carrying a switch, which he handed to the other man with a meaningful gesture. The chief proved to be obliging and promptly dealt him fifty sound strokes, which flayed the skin and caused the blood to flow at every blow. Then, turning to Jim, the chief asked if the whipping had been administered in a way to please him.

Jim denied having wished to see the man whipped. But the chief replied that when one of his followers asked to be punished, he took it for granted that the punishment was deserved, and acted accordingly.

Shortly after returning to the mines Jim could have been on the trail again: his father requested him to go back to the United States to buy some goods, since the workmen preferred wages in goods to payment in money. But Jim, for reasons not revealed, did not desire to make the journey, and Sylvester therefore entrusted the commission to a Spanish clerk, in whom he had great confidence and who set out with thirty thousand dollars in gold en route to Santa Fe and possibly even to St. Louis.

This, though Jim did not yet suspect it, marked one of the great turning points in his life and in his father's. Had he, instead of the Spanish clerk, set out on the purchasing trip, all might have been different. Sylvester might have lived to a prosperous old age, and he himself might have escaped the most harrowing and fateful of all his expeditions.

6

Further Adventures among the Indians

DURING THEIR wanderings, it was inevitable that the Patties should continue to meet Indians, sometimes in friendly contacts, sometimes in armed clashes.

Even when they had no hostile intentions, the trappers sometimes burst forth like fearsome apparitions upon the Indians, who either knew nothing whatever of the whites or had heard of them only in gruesome rumors. Thus one day when they were trapping on a minor tributary of the Gila, they came unexpectedly upon a little band, who fled in terror, not even taking time to save their belongings, which included some rabbitskin robes and a sort of bread made of the sweet bean of the mesquite. In their panic they left a small child behind them; and the infant, says Jim, "screamed so lustily" that they "feared it would have fits," and then did its best to run away from the paleface giants. The giants, however, caught it for its own sake and tied it to a tree so securely that it could not break loose, for they knew that the parents would return for it. Meanwhile they did not loot the Indians' provisions. There were, however, to be occasions when hunger would prevent them from being equally scrupulous.

Next morning two of them returned to the spot and found that the Indians had come back for their possessions, including the child. They had, however, given proof that "the feelings of human nature are the same every where, and that the language of kindness is a universal one; in token of their gratitude, as we understood it, they had suspended a package on a kind of stick, which they had stuck erect." The package contained a large dressed buckskin, which would be most useful for making some needed moccasins. On the stick, by way of a return offering, the Patties tied a red handkerchief, and several days later they found that this handkerchief had been taken.

But evidently, despite this interchange, the Indians had not overcome their dread of the whites, for none of them came to pay a visit.

A little later the wanderers had another near contact with the Indians. Jim had shot a wild goose in the river; and at the report of the gun, women and children began to scream and scrambled away up the mountains, with their men leading the retreat. Hoping to convince the Indians of their amicable intentions, Jim and a mounted companion hastily followed. But a volley of arrows checked their impetuosity, and Jim's companion escaped the darts only after some skillful dodging. Today, as we look back, it is easy to understand the incident: the Indians, seeing two armed white men dashing after them on horseback, naturally thought that their lives were in peril, and struck back in self-defense. But Jim's companion was unable to see things in this clear and simple way. Tired and hungry and in a generally bad mood, he broke out into streams of curses; then, lifting his gun, he was about to shoot one of the Indians, when Jim grabbed the rifle and prevented the murder.

Perhaps it is not surprising that in the Gila country generally the Indians had already learned to dread the white man. Frequently the travelers saw the natives skulking behind them, though their object seems to have been to pick up cast-off bits of meat rather than to start trouble. Meanwhile the actions of the whites did not tend to reassure them. One morning, for example, Sylvester ordered his men to engage in some target practice, forming in line and firing at a certain tree. At the report of their rifles the yells of many Indians—more than a hundred, we are told—shrilled from the mountains above them. The whites tried to make friends of the savages by moving down to the plains and holding out red cloth as an allurement, but the natives refused the bait.

It was not long before the invaders had a clash either with these very Indians or with others like them. They had made camp on the stream; and Jim, whose duty it was to watch the horses that had been penned below, discovered some beavers in a small lake and told his father, who summoned a party to set the traps. Looking down, he saw the horses and mules crowded together, but supposed this only meant that they had eaten enough. But as he stepped into the water to set his traps, he heard a yell from some Indians, of whose presence the Patties had been blithely unaware. Instantly there was a pandemonium of shouts and shots, followed by a rain of arrows; and the horses were seen to be in the power of the raiding savages. Meanwhile Jim and his companions saw six red men sneaking behind them, stopping occasionally, and taking note of everything around. The stalked men promptly hid behind a great cottonwood tree, and each aimed at a separate Indian and fired at the signal of a whistle. Jim's target staggered and dropped, and the others also fell, badly wounded.

Thus far, despite all the arrows, the white men had escaped

injury. But they had fought only the first round of the battle. And except for a lucky chance, the second round might have proved fatal.

The enemy, resorting to an ancient stratagem, had divided their forces, keeping one half on foot and hidden and parading the other half, which consisted of men mounted on the stolen horses. They naturally expected that the infuriated white men would follow these in an effort to regain the animals; and this would give the party in ambush an opportunity to leap out, cut the Patties off from their camp, and catch them between the jaws of a "nutcracker." This ingenious scheme might, as Jim implies, easily have succeeded. But it happened that he, wandering a little distance from camp, came upon some of the ambushed Indians, doubtless as much to their surprise as to his. They set up a yell, and he must have done some deft dodging to escape their arrows. Sylvester, hearing the cries, supposed his son to be encircled and rushed to his aid, only to be met by a shower of arrows, to which he replied with his rifle and pistols, with the result that two Indians fell dead, while the other whites ran to join in the fray. The battle lasted about two hours; but, strangely, we are told of no further casualties.

But though the stratagem of the Indians had failed, the whites did not come out with first honors. Despite some parleying with the Indians, who professed to have attacked them in the mistaken belief that they were Spaniards, they could not recover the missing horses and mules, which, as already mentioned, had been stolen by the savages, and consequently they had to bury the furs, which in turn led to the complete loss of these hard-won and dearly prized possessions.

Their next serious encounter with the Indians occurred after they had returned to the copper mines and were entertaining themselves there at the request of the owner, with no particular occupation except to ward off the savages and hunt wild

animals. One day while in pursuit of deer Jim and two companions came upon the trail of six Indians who were approaching the mines. They quickly abandoned the deer hunt in favor
of a manhunt; and within about a mile of the mines they drew
near the Indians, who, whether or not they had been con-
templating mischief, made every effort to escape. One of them
was surrounded as he tried to dart away into a hollow; and,
seeing two guns cocked and aimed at his face, he threw down
his bow and arrows and pleaded with his pursuers not to shoot
him.

Since he made no hostile move, but crossed his hands and
permitted himself to be tied, they spared his life. And evidently he was grateful for this mercy: after they had gone about
a hundred yards, he returned the favor by saving the lives of
his captors. Pointing to a hollow tree, he made them understand that another Indian lay hidden there with bow and arrows; and on the white men's orders, he called to this man to
come out if he did not wish to be killed. The second Indian
obeyed and was likewise seized and tied. Both Indians were
then marched to the mines and put in jail.

But what was the crime for which they were bound and imprisoned? We are not told but are led to conclude that, since
some Indians had perpetrated outrages, all Indians were suspect, all Indians were treated like the nationals of an enemy
country. More than that, all Indians were in danger of their
lives! "The Spaniards," says Jim, "exasperated with their recent cruelties and murders, would have killed them."

The Patties, on the other hand, insisted on milder methods.
After a night of confinement the prisoners were brought out
and permitted to observe the accuracy of the white men's
target practice. Then one was set free, after being instructed to
tell the chief and all his warriors to come to the mines in order
to make peace. The other was kept as a hostage, under a condition that Jim reports with such matter-of-fact frankness that

one would almost not suppose it to have been cruel or unusual or unjust. If the chief did not come as demanded, the hostage would be slain. More than a century later in the so-called civilized warfare of the world's most technically advanced nations, the slaughter of innocent hostages was to become almost commonplace; but amid the ruder conflicts of the early explorers and trappers, even the threat of this method shocks one, the more so as the whites are the ones responsible. Would they actually have killed the man if the chief had rejected their ultimatum? We do not know. But men of Sylvester's type would surely not have refused any available way of impressing or intimidating their enemies. In this case, however, the point of decision was not reached.

The orders to the released Indian were specific. Within four days four of the whites must meet the chief and his men at a certain hollow within about half a mile of the mines. Otherwise, the hostage—who, incidentally, took the whole matter with the unruffled calm for which his race is noted—would pay with his blood. But why would Sylvester risk four of his men in a conference with a much greater number of presumably treacherous red men? Actually he had no such intention: he had a secret trench dug about a hundred yards from the point of the expected conference, and he filled this trench with armed men, ready for any contingency. Hence he had no reason not to feel confident when sometime before the end of the prescribed four days the parley was held, attended by about eighty Indians.

A council fire had been lit, a pipe and tobacco had been made ready, and a blanket for the chiefs to sit on had been spread on the ground. The four whites then commenced the discussion with four chiefs, who at once declared themselves willing to make peace with the Americans. But with the Spaniards they would never make peace. And why not, the whites wanted to know. Had they themselves never wronged the

Spaniards by taking their horses? Yes, indeed! They admitted many horse thefts, but they went on to charge the Spaniards with a murderous perfidy. One day when the latter had declared themselves eager for peace, a large band of Indians had been lured inside the Spaniards' walls in order to conclude a friendly treaty; and when wholly in the white men's power, they had been massacred like sheep. Only a few had escaped. And these few, swearing everlasting revenge, had repaid treachery with treachery, had gone in among the Spaniards, permitting themselves to be baptized; but all the while they had served as spies for their own people, whom they kept informed as to the best times and places for robbing and killing their enemies.

We have here, of course, only one side of the story; the Spaniards might have had a different tale to tell. But from what we know of the general Spanish attitudes toward the Indians, and from the intensity of the resentment evidently felt by the natives, we may feel reasonably sure that the red men had some genuine, deep-seated grievance.

But against the Americans they had no grievance, and, after being threatened with war by the latter unless they let them operate the mines unmolested, they promised to create no more disturbances. The four chiefs then each in succession made a long speech, which their tribesmen presumably enjoyed more than did their white hearers, who could make out nothing except the words "Americans" and "Española." The orating over, the pipe of peace went the rounds, and a queer ceremony followed: A hole was dug in the ground in the center of the circle of conferees, and each man spat into it. Thereupon the hole was filled, and the warriors danced around it, stuck arrows in the mound above it, covered it with stones, and painted themselves red—all by way of concluding the formalities of peace. The object of spitting into the hole in the ground, they explained, was to bury all their anger and their thoughts of vengeance.

The Indians were naturally frightened when they saw the white men hidden in the trench about a hundred yards away. But they were soon persuaded that the Americans meant them no harm; and thus reassured, they accompanied their new friends to the mines, where three steers were slaughtered to feed them. The head chief then made Sylvester a present of a large tract of land—"ten miles square," says Jim, though ten square miles may have been nearer to the figure, if indeed this was not a great exaggeration. But whatever its size, the land was said to be very fertile. The Spaniards unfortunately had been unable to grow anything on it, owing to the depredations of the Indians, who had killed the farmers or destroyed their crops. But the red men would not molest the Americans; their leader was a "man of truth"; he would not allow the treaty to be violated, and wanted peace with the Americans because they never wished to kill except in battle, as was shown by the fact that they had not slain their two prisoners.

Since an unprecedented peace had now settled down, the Spaniards desired the Patties to remain permanently; the old, bloody strife, they feared, would flare up again the moment they had departed. But Jim, as we have seen, soon wandered away with a band of French trappers, while his father stayed at the mines. After his grim adventure with the Indians who massacred most of the party of Frenchmen, Jim joined another band of whites and proceeded from Indian episode to Indian episode. But not all of the natives were hostile.

Thus, one division of the company came upon some Indians whom Jim calls the "Mokee" (evidently the Hopis). These savages, who seemed never before to have seen a white man, were not at all unfriendly, though they fell flat on the ground in their terror at the sound of a gun. Their weapon was the sling, with which, Jim states, they could kill a deer at a hundred yards.

Equally friendly were the Yumas, whom Jim calls the "Umene." At the junction of the Gila and Colorado rivers they met many of these tribesmen, with whom they conducted a mutually satisfactory trade, giving red cloth in exchange for dried beans. The Indians, who in their native state wore nothing at all, were delighted with the cloth, which they tore into strips and tied about their arms and legs. Jim describes them as "the stoutest men, with the finest forms I ever saw, well proportioned, and as straight as an arrow." However, they had not been content to let nature take its course: the victims of their own peculiar sense of beauty, they had flattened their heads by means of boards that had pressed down their skulls in infancy. "The board is so large and light," Jim continues, "that I have seen women, while swimming the river with their children, towing them after them by a string, which they held in their mouth. The little things neither suffered nor complained, but floated behind their mothers like ducks."

Another tribe of Indians was one which Jim calls the "Cocomarecoppers." Perhaps these had already met some whites, for they turned and fled their wigwams in a panic. But the travelers took care not to harm their possessions, nor to trample their corn, which was knee-high. We are not told whether these Indians or those of another tribe were the ones who visited the company next day at about noon, when it had begun to rain and the white men had pitched their tents and lit their fires. There were about a hundred of them, and they asked for fire, which was given them, enabling them to cook six large beavers, also given them by the white men. Their method was to cover the beavers with dirt and place them in holes in the ground, where they roasted them, entrails and all. That they had had little previous contact with white men was proved by their terror and surprise at gunfire, which made what they called "thunder and lightning."

The next Indians whom the travelers saw were the Mohaves, whose name Jim gives as "Mohawa." These Indians, like the Cocomarecoppers, were alarmed to see the strangers. The women and children screamed and hid in their huts while the intruders thrust their way through the village—which is hardly surprising, for would we ourselves not be alarmed if an army of fierce-looking foreigners, clad in a strange garb and unlike any persons we had ever seen before, should suddenly come trooping past our homes?

Nevertheless, the men of the tribe were not intimidated. About a hundred of them followed the whites to their camping place three miles above the village, and the chief, "a dark and sulky looking savage," made signs that he wanted the gift of a horse. This gift, according to his reasoning, was due him: by pointing to the river and to the furs that the trappers had gathered, he made signs that these were his and that he deserved to be paid for the riches taken from his territory. After all, did his arguments not have a certain plausibility? If uninvited aliens began hunting in the white man's land, would they not be asked, at the very least, to make some compensation?

But the intruders did not see things in this way. Inevitably they refused the chief's request, with the result that he drew himself up sternly and fiercely, uttered his war whoop, and drove an arrow into a tree. One of the whites then shot the arrow in two, which startled the chief so much that he left with his men. But next morning, after the whites had hastily fortified their camp in fear of a night attack, he returned and again asked for a horse. As before, he was refused, apparently with great abruptness; and in his anger he galloped away and drove a spear through one of the horses tied not far from the camp.

Immediately vengeance was followed by countervengeance.
Before the chief had raced another fifty yards, four rifle shots
rang out, and he went plummeting from his horse.

The irrational nature of the exchange is highlighted by
Jim's next statement: "We could not doubt, that the Indians
would attempt to revenge the death of their chief." If the men
had no doubt on this subject, why, in the name of common
prudence, had they killed the chief? Was it their desire to
provoke a blood feud? Or had they, like the Indian himself,
merely acted in a frenzy of passion? The fact that he was, as
Jim says, "pierced by four bullets," shows that the attack did
not spring from the ungovernable impulse of a single maniac.
The truth is that we have here an example of the savage emo-
tionalism and equally savage intolerance in which small wars
and great have originated.

Subsequent events made it all the clearer that the whole
episode was as senseless as it was bloody and brutal. Foreseeing
an attack, the white men felt obliged to build breastworks and
to post observers high in the trees in order to spy out any approaching Indians. None appeared, however, during the day
or night, but in the morning the whites were saluted with a
shower of arrows, followed by a war whoop and a charge of
warriors. These were halted with rifle balls, which brought
some of them low; and immediately the defenders surged out
after the Indians and killed sixteen in all. Truly the blood
feud was proceeding in high gear!

But no one could have expected that this would be the end.
The company moved on as rapidly as they could, and every
night they fortified their camp. Yet they did not blame their
own actions for this necessity. Jim could naively remark that
"these red children of the desert . . . appear to inherit an equal
hatred of all whites." In view of the murder of the chief, the
word "inherit" would hardly seem appropriate.

However, there can be no question that the hatred did exist. And it burst forth one night when, exhausted after four restless days, the men had fallen asleep around their fires without taking the precaution to build breastworks and without posting more than one guard. The Indians, no doubt following at a safe distance, saw this as their heaven-given opportunity and struck with a rain of arrows which killed two men and wounded two. They then vanished in the night before anyone could fire back.

Jim himself had the narrowest of escapes. One of the slain men had been sleeping beside him, and his own hunting shirt was transfixed by two arrows. Sixteen arrows were sticking out of his blanket, some of them nailing it to the ground.

The second round in the blood feud must, therefore, be scored in favor of the Indians.

The third round began next morning, after the white survivors had passed a sleepless night, with their fires extinguished. None of them seems to have questioned that the proper thing now was to go out and shoot some more Indians. Eighteen avengers took the trail and soon came upon the savages, who were making a meal of horsemeat. They fled, however, before their assailants came within rifle range, but the latter put spurs to their horses and overtook them just as they sought refuge in a thicket, and killed a large number. They were, Jim says, "a division of the band" that had attacked them—which may easily have been true, though by what clairvoyant vision did Jim know this? The attack, one must remember, had been launched in the dark. But the attackers were merely being true to the time-hallowed traditions of the blood feud, which never squeamishly limits its victims to the guilty. That the killers were thinking mainly of vengeance is shown by the fact that they hung the bodies of the slain from the limbs of trees, where they might "dangle in terror to the rest."

Now, as they traveled on, the adventurers had brushes with the members of various other tribes. In one case they encountered a small band, whose men fled, gallantly leaving one isolated woman behind. Unable to escape, she beat her breast and cried, "*Cowera! Cowera!*" which may have been the name of her tribe. But they "treated her kindly," says Jim, and pressed on their way. A little later they came to a village of the Shuena, who greeted them with arrows, which were returned with a rain of bullets. A revealing passage in the *Personal Narrative* unbares with unadorned frankness the attitude of the intruders:

> In the excitement of an attack, we laughed heartily to see these sons of the desert dodge, and skulk away half bent, as though the heavens were falling upon them. From their manner we inferred, that they were in fact wholly unacquainted with white people, or at least they never before heard the report of a gun.

Doubtless it was highly amusing to see the Indians skulking and running away in the attempt to save their lives—just as amusing as it would be to see a man fall downstairs and break his leg, which would likewise cause amusement to a certain type of mind.

In this comical affair, to be sure, some of the Indians lost their lives—how many, we do not know, for Jim notes this trivial detail only in passing. "The whole establishment," he goes on to say, "dispersed to the mountains, and we marched through the village without seeing any inhabitants, except the bodies of those we had killed."

No wonder, however, that they moved on "with great circumspection" and consumed so much time with questions of attack and defense and with fortification of their camps that they "had little leisure to trap." Even from the practical point of view of the hunt for furs, the blood feud seems not to have been profitable.

They were, as it happened, far from finished with the blood feud; if they were willing to call an end to the slaughter, their enemies were not. This was tragically impressed upon them one day when, having reached a small tributary of the Colorado, they sent three men ahead with traps in search of beavers. Next day the prospectors had not returned at the appointed time, nor did they come back during the following twenty-four hours. Their comrades naturally were worried and set out to discover what had happened. The search was all too successful: they did find the men—cut into pieces, and spitted before a fire like beavers roasting.

Their feelings toward the Indians, in the light of this grim episode, can well be imagined. And apparently it was these same exascerbated feelings that took command sometime later when, after threading the Grand Canyon of the Colorado, they encountered a large band of Shoshone Indians, who, Jim would have us believe, were in the habit of killing white people after feigning friendship. These Shoshones wore buffalo robes and carried muskets—firearms that, says Jim, "they must have taken from the white people." This statement, however, gives rise to some questions: How did Jim know that the possessors had not obtained the weapons in legitimate trading? And if they had originally had only bows and arrows, how had they been able to take the guns from the whites?

The *Personal Narrative* proceeds with this sentence, which reveals most by what it does not say: "We demanded them to give up the fire arms, which they refused."

Why, they must have asked themselves, should they strip themselves defenseless? And what right had the arrogant strangers to their guns? But the strangers, having been rebuffed by the inevitable "No!" went on to act as they thought proper for the born lords of the land. "On this," writes Jim, "we gave them our fire, and they fled to the mountains." Their women and children were left behind in the power of the invaders, who, however, magnanimously "had no disposition to harm them"—that is, not at first. This clement attitude disappeared a little later, when they found six scalps, which the women declared to be those of French hunters. This, adds Jim, in as matter-of-fact a way as if the announcement were only to be expected, "so exasperated us, that we hardly refrained from killing the women."

But they did not, so far as we are told, stoop to this crowning barbarity, though they did loot the village of all the beaver skins taken from the slain Frenchmen, along with five mules and a supply of dried buffalo meat. And now, almost casually, in the way of one who adds a minor detail as an afterthought, Jim mentions another fact a little out of chronological order: "We had killed eight of their men."

A strange side commentary is that the massacre of the Shoshones was as pleasing to certain other Indians as to the whites themselves. If the Indians had been able to band together, forming themselves into a great confederacy under an able common leader and not wasting their blood in intertribal affrays, surely the invaders would have found much more formidable barricades imposed against them, and might have been much slower in overrunning the land. But once more—as when the Pawnees and their tribal enemies had exulted in taking each other's scalps—we find the red man playing the white man's game. Reaching a village of the Navahos, who were friendly to the whites, the wanderers reported how many Shoshones they had killed; and the Navahos, being at war with the Shoshones, expressed their delight, and rewarded the whites with one horse in return for each dead Shoshone, and furthermore dispatched scouts to show them the way across the mountains.

In the course of the next month or two, the trappers met two other tribes, including some of the "Grasshopper Indians," who had earned their name from their practice of making a sort of bread from dried and pulverized grasshoppers. These savages, on seeing the palefaces, "dodged into the high

grass like so many partridges." They were fortunate in not being shot down like partridges.

But a little later the travelers came upon a more formidable
party, some mounted Blackfeet warriors, who rushed upon
them, "yelling as though the spirit of darkness had loaned
them the voices of all his tenants." This naturally resulted in
a battle, partly at close range, which lasted about twenty minutes; and finally the Blackfeet fled, so swiftly that it was impossible to catch up with them. On the field behind them, they
had left sixteen of their dead, side by side with four dead white
men.

Regarding the latter, Jim bursts out in a feeling passage:

We buried them with sorrowful hearts, and eyes full of tears.
Ah! Among those who live at home, surrounded by numerous
relations and friends, in the midst of repose, plenty, and security,
when one of their number droops, and dies with sickness or age,
his removal leaves a chasm that is not filled for years. Think
how we must have mourned these brave men, who had shared
so many dangers, and on whose courage and aid we had every
day relied for protection. Here on these remote plains, far from
their friends, they had fallen by the bloody arrow or spear of
those red, barbarous Ishmaelites of the desert.

Thus, even amid sorrow over fallen companions, the bitterness against the Indian manifests itself. But no doubt such
bitterness was only natural to a man who had just seen his
friends struck down.

On a subsequent expedition Jim was once more lucky to
escape with his life. He had grown tired of the routine at the
mines and, much against his father's wishes, had joined a band
of fifteen men who planned to trap on the Puerco River of
New Mexico, which joins the Rio del Norte near Socorro,
New Mexico; in evident confusion, he calls it the "Pacos."
There he had the gloomy experience of traveling through a
plain dotted with deserted cottages and forsaken sheepfolds

and horse pens—a fair and fertile region which testified to the bitterness of the feud between the Spaniards and the Indians, whose raids had compelled the settlers to abandon the entire region. But it would not be long before Jim's party and the savages had their own contacts.

One day after their sentinels had warned them of Indians, they had barely time to take shelter behind trees before being attacked with arrows. They replied with gunfire, killing a number of red men; but this did not put an end to the assault, which continued from all directions, until it became difficult for the whites to dodge. After a time one of them was struck down, and the Indians scurried forward to take his scalp. In the effort to prevent this atrocity Jim dashed from behind a tree, but was met with a hail of arrows, which he tried to avoid, without complete success, for an excruciating pain in his hip told him that he had been hit. Had a timely shot from his companions not struck down some of the Indians as they rushed toward him, he would, as he says, have been instantly killed.

A lull in the attack enabled him to pull the arrow out of his hip. But before he could reload his gun, a second arrow smote him under the right breast, though it was less painful than the first dart. Not being able to draw it out, he snapped it off, reloaded his gun, and hobbled away, while the nearest Indian fell dead. Despite the great numerical superiority of the attackers, he and his comrades managed to gain shelter beneath the riverbank, where they were safe from arrows. One white man had been killed, and one in addition to Jim was wounded, though not seriously, while the Indians had lost twenty-eight men and gained nothing except a few blankets which they took in the course of their flight. A comment on the ferocity of the fight, and on the savagery of the passions that it aroused even in white breasts, is to be found in a sentence regarding the dead and wounded enemies: "Truth is, we were too much exasperated to show mercy, and we cut off the heads of all, in-discriminately."

Jim now had to submit to the rudest of surgery, without benefit of anesthetics or antiseptics, while a companion took several minutes to remove the fragment of arrow from his breast. The arrow in his hip could not be entirely withdrawn, for it was of flint, and, though he does not state whether it left any aftereffects, it had slivered against the bone.

The attacking Indians, whom he calls the "Muscallaros," were "admirably formed, with fine features and a bright complexion inclining to yellow." Their long black hair hung in braids about their shoulders, sometimes almost down to their knees; they wore buckskin belts about the waist, with matching jackets and moccasins; and their appearance in battle, when fully painted, was "most formidable."

Once more the party had proof of the antagonism of Indian against Indian. Meeting a party of Navahos, who were engaged in a blood feud with the Muscallaros because of the killing of one of their men, the trappers displayed the scalps of the dead Muscallaros. The result was a series of "frantic leaps and gestures of joy," and "screams and yells of exultation . . . as though a whole bedlam had broke loose." After the medicine man had eased the pain of Jim's wounds by applying a poultice of a content unknown to him, the tribesmen engaged in the fiercest dancing and singing he had ever seen. For three days and nights the celebration continued; and meanwhile the white men "endured a sort of worship from them, particularly the women," and were continually being treated to the Navahos' favorite dishes.

The ceremonies over, the tribesmen accompanied their new-won friends back to the scene of the battle with the Muscallaros and took great pleasure in the sight of their slain enemies. But they manifested deep respect when shown the burial place of the white man killed in the conflict, and walked about the grave solemnly, chanting funeral songs. Each of them left a gift at the grave, "some an arrow, others meat, moccasins, tobacco, war-feathers, and the like, all articles of value to them." For the Indians, like many peoples throughout the world—even civilized peoples, such as the ancient Sumerians and Egyptians—believed that the dead in their afterlife had need of the physical objects that had served them on earth, and were ready and even lovingly eager to sacrifice these needed articles for the benefit of their spirits.

7

The Swallowing Wilderness

When Sylvester Pattie decided to settle down at the copper mines, undoubtedly he was governed in part by a knowledge of the hazardous life of hunters, trappers, and wanderers in the wilderness. We of today in our secure and guarded existence, with an assurance of adequate food, water, and medical and hospital care and with no wild beasts or still wilder men menacing us in bloody raids, can have little idea of the precarious nature of life in the early west. But some suggestion of the reality, when sickness, accident, and death were always next-door neighbors, may be gleaned from a statement in the *Personal Narrative*.

Early in 1827, barely more than two and a half years after the start of his adventures, Jim met some of his companions of the Pratte expedition. Inevitably he asked about the others, but the news he received was most disheartening. Of the hundred and sixteen men who had left the United States in 1824, some had fallen beneath gunfire or arrows, and others, including Pratte himself, had died of disease; out of the entire company not more than sixteen remained alive!

This statement, to be sure, may be an exaggeration; even for those turbulent times the death rate seems excessive. One suspects that some of the news may have been false, and that some men who were merely unreported were listed as dead. But whether or not the statement was accurate in all its details, certainly it was true as to many of the company, some of whom, such as its organizer, were definitely known to have died. We may be certain that the mortality rate among the adventurers was such that no insurance company would have accepted them as good risks.

Sylvester, therefore, seems to have been well advised to remain at the mines. There he might have led a comfortable life of normal length and might have prospered and grown rich, had fate not seized him, as it were, by the scruff of the neck and thrown him out again upon the long, hard trail.

We have seen how he had requested Jim to travel to the United States in order to purchase some goods, and how, Jim having refused, he had entrusted the mission to a Spanish clerk in whom he had great confidence. That confidence must have been unusually strong—or perhaps Sylvester, like many another honest man, had an excessive faith in human nature. To send a clerk, with thirty thousand dollars in gold, into a remote wilderness where he could disappear without much danger of being apprehended, was certainly to dangle a severe temptation before his eyes. Even if he had been dependable in small matters, in which nothing very much was at stake, did it follow that he could resist the lure of ill-gotten sudden riches?

Apparently the man's general reputation had been good. Jim tells us that when he went on his way, "he left none behind to doubt his truth and honor, nor was there the least suspicion of him." But suspicion could not help growing when the time for a letter came and brought no word. "A dim surmise," says Jim, "began then to grow up, that he had run off with the money." This "dim surmise" apparently became much less dim when further time went by without any news. The explanation, of course—though Jim does not mention this possibility—may not have been that the man was dishonest, but that he had fallen in with bandits, who had stripped him of his money and abandoned his body in some remote gulch.

Whatever the cause of his silence, Jim was dispatched to hunt for the missing clerk. But from the beginning he felt the search to be hopeless, as the Spaniard had not only had a month's head start, but was a person of "infinite ingenuity," who could speak Russian and French as well as Spanish and English and would therefore find it the easier to hide his tracks.

Jim's inquiries, as he had foreseen, brought no result. As he returned to the mines, he was scourged by pangs of remorse at having refused to undertake the purchasing journey at his father's request; he truly suffered torments for, as he tells us, "There is no misery like self-condemnation." He does not even consider that if he had gone on the trip, he might only have made things worse for his father, since he, instead of the clerk, might have been robbed and murdered.

Now where there had been a prospect of success, if not of opulence, he could see only poverty and misfortune staring at him. But he assures us that his grief was not for himself, but "for my father and his companions, who had toiled by day and night with unwearied assiduity, to accumulate something for their dear and helpless families, whom they had left in Missouri." In particular, he thought of his own seven younger brothers and sisters.

We might expect that the loss, though great, would not in the course of time have proved irreparable. But at this point destiny tied one of her cruel knots. On visiting the

owner of the mines, whom he sought out in a last despairing
effort to locate the Spanish clerk, Jim received a new blow.
An order had just been issued by the President of Mexico requiring all persons born in old Spain to leave the country, with
but a month in which to settle their affairs. This order unfortunately applied to the owner of the mines, who confessed
to Jim his hope that Sylvester would buy the property. To
Sylvester, who would have been assured of an adequate income
for the rest of his days, this would have been the opportunity
of a lifetime—if he had still had the thirty thousand dollars
that he had entrusted to the Spanish clerk. But without the
money the purchase would be out of the question.

In company with the owner Jim returned to the mines,
where Sylvester heard the sad news that the property must be
sold for whatever could be obtained for it and that he would
have to leave. Once more, therefore, Sylvester was thrown
back upon his own resources. And since a man usually follows
the lines of his experience, he broke his resolution to lead a
settled life and once more became a trapper. He and his son
hastened to Santa Fe, and there after a wait of about twelve
days they joined a company of thirty men, with the intention
of trapping on the Colorado, and obtained a passport to
enter the provinces of Chihuahua and Sonora. Of this company, Sylvester was chosen the captain.

Finding few beavers on the Gila, where they had already
been trapped almost to the point of extinction, the party
pushed on to the so-called Beaver River, where the animals
were more abundant. And now Sylvester, "to prevent the
disagreement and insubordination which are apt to spring up
in these associations," drew up some extraordinary papers,
which all the men signed. They were to trap in partnership,
but any of them who disobeyed their commander would be
tried by a jury of his comrades and, if declared guilty, would
pay a fine of fifty dollars in furs. So far, so good! But if any

man tried to desert the party, his punishment would be truly Draconian: he would be shot.

At this point the narrator provides a long and illuminating explanation of the necessity for such measures. He tells us that the trappers, when bound by no power from above, were certain to break up into smaller bands, which would fall an easy prey to the Indians. Men of all types and moods were thrown together; and beneath the trials of the camp, facing the hard labor of cooking, standing guard, or throwing up breastworks, while perhaps hungry, naked, and exhausted, they might be surly and quarrelsome. But an even worse source of dissension lay in the fact that individuals were greatly uneven in their trapping abilities; three or four experts might catch as many beavers as an ill-assorted party of thirty; and such a group of three or four, with a sense of its own superiority, might break off from the others, with results that Jim feelingly explains:

Sad experience has made me acquainted with all these causes of disunion and dissolution of such companies. I have learned them by wounds and suffering, by toil and danger of every sort, by wandering about in the wild and desolate mountains, alone and half starved, merely because two or three bad men had divided our company, strong and sufficient to themselves in union, but miserable, and exposed to almost certain ruin in separation.

Even admitting these facts and the peril to all if the company were divided, could any good results be expected from a compact such as Sylvester had drawn up? Could mere signatures on paper hold down a group of self-willed and reckless characters? And if they broke their agreement, would the leader or any of his henchmen actually go to the dread extreme of shooting the rebels? More than that, if they did shoot the deserters, would that not be murder by the laws of any country, regardless of any compacts signed? But strange, very strange, even if not always exactly legal, are the agreements drawn up by adventurers in the wilderness. The papers signed by Pattie's followers are surely not half so wild or irrational as others known to history, such as the famous document made three centuries before by the trio of rogues, Pizarro, Almagro, and the priest De Luque, who agreed before a notary to divide among themselves the loot of the still unexplored continent of South America.

The contract, as it turned out, could not save Pattie's party from almost immediate trouble. Lack of provisions—never in any circumstances a unifying element—plagued them almost from the beginning—which may mean that the region had already been so thoroughly hunted and trapped that little game remained. The men were reduced to killing and eating their dogs and then six of their horses. And this, to Jim, was "the most cruel task of all."

It is a curious fact that this hunter and trapper, who had killed innumerable animals apparently without compunction and even for the pleasure of destroying them, was moved almost to tears at the thought of shooting his horse, which, he says, "had borne us over deserts and mountains, as hungry as ourselves, and strongly and faithfully attached to us." "I loved this horse," he goes on to relate, "and he seemed to have an equal attachment for me. When I held up the bridle toward him, I could see consent and good will in his eye."

But it is with animals as with men: those which we know and live with we grow to love, for we recognize them as individuals, see their good qualities, and develop sympathy for them and a fellow feeling. But those whom we observe only from far off, we do not identify as individuals, nor as the possessors of any good qualities; hence their death—whether it occurs in hunting or in warfare—causes us no pang.

Though it had fallen to Jim's lot to kill his horse, he could not bear to fire his gun at the animal, which gazed at him "with a look of steady kindness." His head whirled, he became dizzy, his gun fell, and, after recovering himself, he offered a beaver skin to anyone who would perform the grim task for him. At this price he soon found a substitute.

By means of the horsemeat and the flesh of an occasional deer or wolf, the party managed to remain alive. But dissension was inevitable. The split occurred over the question of the proposed route: most of the men decided that the contemplated course, down the Gila to its mouth and then up the Colorado, was too long and would involve too much danger from too many Indians. Therefore they decided to seek the Colorado by a shortcut overland. However, what about their compact?

One can imagine that some hot words passed back and forth when the men denied being bound by the agreement. There was unfortunately nothing that Sylvester could do, except to storm and plead. The dissenters had the supreme argument on their side—they were in the majority. Regardless of signed documents, six or eight men do not attempt to shoot twenty-two or twenty-four armed comrades.

At first, indeed, Sylvester seemed in danger of being deserted by everyone except his son. But two hired men, whom he was ready to pay and dismiss, decided that they would be safer with him than with the other group; and four more, after hearing the hired men's arguments, came over to the leader's side and were received as partners. This gave eight in all for the Patties' company. The compact was now so far forgotten that when the moment of parting arrived, the men all shook hands and exchanged hearty good wishes.

New pledges, however, were taken by the remaining eight, who solemnly swore to hold together until the death. Now, of necessity, being but a small group, they advanced with painstaking caution, tying their horses every night and camping close to them. From numerous footprints, as well as from the smoke of campfires to the north, they knew that the Indians were near. And they took it for granted that the savages were hostile.

Nevertheless they did meet some apparently friendly natives, of a tribe that Jim calls the "Umeas" (evidently one of his ways of spelling "Yumas"). Some of these, who could speak Spanish, were unwittingly to bring great misfortune on the party by giving false information as to the source of the cloth they wore about their loins. This, they reported, came from the Christians of the California coast; and when the Patties asked if there were any Christians living on the Colorado River, they answered in the affirmative, perhaps actually believing what they said and no better able than the white men to realize what damage could spring from a simple misstatement.

Although the Yumas seemed well disposed, sad experience had taught the whites "that caution is the parent of security" and left them far from pleased when more than two hundred red men swam the river to visit them. The numbers of these new friends awed them. "In the midst of these multitudes of fierce, naked, swarthy savages," reports Jim, "eight of us seemed no more than a little patch of snow on the side of one of the black mountains." There may be a minor inconsistency in the description, since Jim calls the natives both "fierce" and "friendly." But inconsistent or not, he and his comrades took no chances: they permitted only a few Indians at a time to approach them, and these had first to put aside their arms. Though we are told of no menacing incident, we need not read between the lines in order to get a sense of the tenseness, the anxiety behind Jim's statement that "We were perfectly aware how critical was our position."

Even had the writer not been so explicit, we might conjecture the men's feelings from the fact that they marched sixteen miles that evening before camping on the riverbank. Their camping place was a plain, where the grass grew headhigh, providing a suitable spot in which to tie the horses. Owing to the late hour they did not make a pen for the animals, nor protect themselves with breastworks. But it is questionable whether such precautions would have helped much, considering that the night was stormy and so dark that the men could not see their own hands before them.

Two sentinels were posted to guard the horses from possible Indian attack. And the other six wanderers, warmed by whatever fires they could keep burning, lay down to sleep beside their wet blankets. In a short while they were awakened by the snorting of the mules and horses, and sprang up in alarm, put out the fires, and went groping through the pitchy gloom. But they could discover nothing amiss; seemingly the disturbance had been caused by a prowling bear or other wild beast. And so, perhaps cursing and grumbling a bit, they relit the fires.

But there was to be little sleep for them that night. Suddenly a yell burst through the darkness—a sound they know too well, the whooping of Indians. At the same time, as if to provide a suitable stage setting, the rain began pouring down again, the wind tore past them with howling gusts, the lightning flared fitfully, and the thunder crashed about them.

Simultaneously, while the cries of the Indians still rang out yell on yell, the men heard a clattering of hoofs and realized that the mules and horses were loose. The Indians, creeping up in the dark with a catlike power of seeing where white eyes were blind, had untied all the animals! With a ferocious clamoring they were driving the terrified beasts away!

But what could the white men do to halt them? Though they could see nothing, they rushed out after the marauders, and "fired at the noises," which could hardly have harmed the noise makers. To intercept them, to stop them, appeared impossible, the more so as the thieves might have been joined by mounted tribesmen. Gradually the cries grew remote, the clattering of hoofs died away, and the eight white men were alone with the night and the storm.

Their position now was desperate beyond imagining. In the heart of an inhospitable wilderness, hundreds of miles from any white settlement in a country populated only by savages, they had lost their means of mobility, their means of transportation. Not a single beast remained to carry their goods or themselves! And to lose one's horse, in the eyes of the old west, was rightly regarded as one of the worst of misfortunes—this was why horse theft was ordinarily punished by death.

Seated about a great fire, the robbed men bleakly discussed their predicament. But what could they do? Their first thought was to follow on the trail of the thieves and try to regain the stolen animals or else die in the attempt. But if they could neither recover the animals nor draw the Indians into a last-ditch battle, they might swim the river, attack the native town, and kill as many of the people as they could. These suggestions, voiced by Sylvester, were endorsed by all his followers. It is indicative of their bitterness that, in the way of Indian vengeance-seekers, they were willing to strike alike at the guilty and at the guiltless, at armed men and at women and children.

In the morning they set out after the robbers, but soon discovered that the Indians had divided into several bands and vanished with the horses into the mountain canyons, where there was no way to follow them. The whites therefore

turned to the second part of their plan, and after a meal of
beaver meat they swam the river, pushing rafts on which they
had tied their guns. In the early afternoon they reached the
village and strode up to it with the courage of hopelessness,
only to find it unoccupied except for one white-haired man,
so blind and deaf that, like the old grandfather Jim came
upon in another village in an earlier day, he seemed not even
aware of their arrival. The savagery of their feelings is eloquent
in Jim's statement that "Our exasperation of despair inclined
us to kill even him." But Sylvester, more merciful than his
followers, vetoed the idea. The men then set fire to the village,
burning every hut except that which sheltered the old man.
And having reduced the place to ashes, they swam back
across the river and returned to their camp.

But though the acts of revenge may have provided a balm
for their outraged feelings, what actually had they accomplished except to assure the enmity of the entire Indian tribe?
Surely not every inhabitant of the village had been involved
in the horse thefts, which were probably unknown to many.
Then why had the Indians abandoned the village? Because,
as Jim explains, they were frightened by the white men, who
were so unfamiliar to them that they would fall flat on the
ground at the sound of gunfire and, upon rising, would want
to take flight.

Despite the destruction of the village, the situation of the
whites was exactly what it had been at the moment of the
loss of the horses. They were still marooned deep in an unknown and dangerous wilderness, without means of getting to
the nearest civilized settlement and even without knowledge
of where such a settlement might be.

Now in their despair how they must have regretted that
they had not set off with the other twenty-two men in the
attempted shortcut across the desert—though who knew what

terrifying adventures the others might not have encountered? And now they would have to draw upon every resource of skill and ingenuity ever called forth in a dire emergency by the most intrepid of frontiersmen.

8

Flood and Thirst

FOR A substitute means of transportation, the eight stranded adventurers grasped at the obvious. In all ages and in most lands the rivers have provided some of man's chief highways; and the broad Colorado, flowing steadily to the south, offered an invitation and a temptation. Where did it lead? They did not know. But they had been told by the Indians about Christian—in other words, Spanish—settlements along its banks; and they congratulated themselves on having obtained the information, although their motive in inquiring had been mere curiosity. If any doubt concerning the reliability of the report seeped into their minds, Jim does not mention it. Besides, why cloud the one avenue of hope when everything else was blank with despair?

They thought it fortunate that they had all the tools necessary for making canoes, and all the materials in the trees of the riverbank. Their only apprehension was that the Indians might attack them before the work was completed; and they began, accordingly, by erecting a sort of fort, and then set to work among the trees, while a sentry high up in the branches kept constant watch for approaching red men. None appeared, however, and the work on the canoes continued until eight in all had been launched. These, when joined in pairs by means of platforms, were sufficient to carry not only the men but all their traps and furs. But there was no room for the saddles, which the men hid; it was their hope to buy horses at the Spanish settlements and recover the saddles when passing back this way.

At about four miles an hour they floated downstream. And after passing the smoldering ruins of the Indian village, they trapped great numbers of beavers, apparently never pausing to consider that in their position nothing could be less important than wealth in beaver skins. It is indicative of their greed for these riches that after going sixty or seventy miles they had so many furs that they had to build more canoes to carry the booty. Truly it was as if a group of Crusoes, lost on unknown shores and faced with the threat of death, had blandly overlooked their peril while accumulating pearls and gold.

Not until three days after starting on their canoe trip, did they have their first sight of Indians. By accident, about thirty miles below the burnt village they detected two Indians poised with bows and arrows in a tree near the riverbank. And instantly—by what logic we are not told, since these savages might have been looking for game or for other Indians—the voyagers concluded that the men were waiting for them, hoping to slay them with arrows as they passed. Apparently they did not ask why, if the Indians had planned to attack them from the trees, they had waited so long before launching the assault, nor why the blow was being aimed at a point thirty miles below the burnt village; nor did they pause to consider that the men in the trees might not be Yumas at all.

But terror provides its own arguments. From a range of a little under a hundred yards, Sylvester and one of his followers fired into the trees and brought two Indians down with a sound that reminded Jim "exactly of the fall of a bear or a turkey." Fearing that the slain two might be members of a larger band, the white men then crossed the river, and some of them climbed trees, from which they could scan both banks. But finding no signs of other Indians, they recrossed the stream and inspected the bodies of their victims, whom they concluded to be members of the party that had stolen the horses, since they wore some of the horses' hempen ropes about their waists.

Having mentioned that they "hung the bodies of the thieves from a tree, with the product of their own thefts," Jim proceeds to some moralizing. He tells us that he and his comrades were "much relieved" to discover that the slain Indians were really the horse thieves; and thus, unconsciously he shows that they had had some hearty doubts and perhaps even some hidden compunctions. "Though none of us felt any particular forbearance toward Indians under any circumstances," the report goes on, "it certainly would have pained us to have killed Indians that had never disturbed us."

After passing through a country inhabited by foxes, wildcats, pumas, jaguars, wild geese, pelicans, and large numbers of other birds, they came upon ten Indians on a sandbank. Dark-skinned and naked, and with heads shaved except for tufts of hair which stood erect as sticks on their scalps, they were of a tribe (the Cocopas) then unknown to the travelers; and they fled at their first glimpse of the white men. But the Patties wished very much to speak with them, for they were worried about not having seen the expected Spanish settlements and, fearing that they had missed them, were eager for directions.

Three days passed before they could approach any of the

Cocopas. Then early one morning they discovered some wigwams near the river's edge, with some families in them, still
asleep. On seeing the whites—who must have looked like
apparitions out of some other world, with their tall, powerful
frames, their light skins, buckskin clothing, and beards—the
Cocopas were "apparently frightened to insanity," the women
and children "screaming as if going into convulsions." Presumably they had been surrounded, or else had been paralyzed
into inaction, for they made little effort to escape.

But the whites, by offering them meat and making signs
that they wished to smoke with them, gradually overcame
their dread. The women and children, at a word from the men,
ceased their fearful clamoring, the pipe of peace was lit, and
the Indians began striking themselves on the breast and fore-
head, apparently in appeal to One on high. "It showed more
like reverence to him," says Jim, "than any thing we had yet
seen among the Indians; though I have seen none but what
admit that there is a master of life, which they call by a name
to that import, or that of a Great Spirit."

The ensuing conversation was a most uncertain one, conducted in the sign language. Wishing to know how far it was
to the supposed Spanish settlements, the white men drew the
images of domestic animals such as cows and sheep in the
sand, for it was reasonable to suppose that these creatures
would be present at the settlements. And they thought that the
Cocopas understood, for the latter pointed to the west and
then at the travelers' clothes and at their bare skins, which
led the Patties to believe that other white men dwelt farther
to the west. Actually, of course, this conclusion may have
been quite unjustified; the Indians may even have imagined
that the drawings, whose subjects they probably could not
identify, represented some sort of religious ceremonial or
magical rite.

The visitors next made gestures to ask if the Indians had

ever seen palefaces before (though the reception they had had should have provided them with the answer). But they gathered that while these particular natives had never seen any white men, nevertheless their chief down the river had seen such persons.

The trappers now gave some shirts to the Indian women, who were entirely naked. But these ladies, many of whom were no more than sixteen years old and had "the most perfect figures" Jim had ever seen— "the hair of some hanging nearly to their heels"—were complete strangers to the white man's prudery and could not even understand that clothes were meant to be worn. As for the men, they were most interested in their visitors' firearms, particularly when Jim, as a demonstration, shot a wild goose in the river. At the discharge the Cocopas all fled into the bushes, though some in their terror first fell flat on the ground; and it was some time before they could be coaxed out again.

After leaving gifts of beaver meat and bidding the Indians a friendly farewell, the party drifted down the river to the abode of the Cocopa chief. This dignitary, who had been advised of their coming, had prepared a feast—that is, a feast according to his own lights, for the pièce de résistance consisted of fatted dog. But the guests knew enough not to refuse anything offered them in hospitality; and so they ate the dog meat just as if it had been beef.

First, however, they had to listen to a long speech in the Indian dialect, which they understood not at all. But they did understand the gestures of the chief when the repast was over, and when, puffing out his belly and striking it with one hand, he asked the diners if they had had enough. They likewise understood when he uttered the names of several Indian tribes, with the evident idea of asking how the travelers had fared among them. Observing his glowering looks upon their reference to the Yumas, they knew that he was at war with these people. He pointed to two small children, crying, "Yuma! Yuma!"—thus showing that, unlike the Pawnees, his people did not truss up and sacrifice small prisoners of war. But he behaved exactly like other warlike Indians when, being shown the scalps of the two Yumas who had been shot in the trees of the riverbank, he seized the grisly relics in his teeth and shook them like a dog shaking a rat, then yelled in delight, summoning his people to do a dance of rejoicing. "Their deportment," says Jim, ". . . was in fact much nearer bestial than human. They would leave the dance round the scalps in turn, to come and caress us, and then return and resume the dance."

Doubtless Jim did not realize that the dancing, yelling, and general cavorting were unconscious means of whipping up warlike emotions and, in effect, of carrying on and inflaming the feud with the Yumas.

But the one thing that really interested the white men was information about other whites. From the fact that the chief "made a very tolerable imitation of the rolling and breaking of the surf on the sea shore," and from the further fact that he drew what they took to be a sheep and a cow, they were convinced that there were Spanish settlements at no great distance to the west.

Thus reassured, they continued on their way down the river. Some distance below the Cocopa village, they had another of those senseless, bloody conflicts with which the *Personal Narrative* abounds. Some Indians, against whom they had been warned (of a tribe which Jim calls the "Pipis"), shot at the travelers with arrows as they floated downstream, but did them no direct harm, as they were able to pull out of range to the opposite bank. Obviously they might have kept on their way without making any demonstration and might soon have left the hostile savages well behind them. Or else, if they felt it necessary to intimidate the aggressors, they could have accomplished this purpose by aiming a few shots above their heads. But no! The attitude of the whites bristles in Jim's statement: "We sprang upon the bank, took fair aim, and showed them the difference between their weapons and ours, by leveling six of them."

As they drifted downstream, the wanderers found that the fur of the captured beavers became shorter and thus less valuable; and many raccoons annoyed them by inconsiderately getting caught "instead of the true game." Finally the movement of the river seemed to cease entirely. And while they were puzzling over the cause, the current resumed, at the increased rate of six miles an hour—which was the first time that any of the party had ever come under the influence of the ocean tides. Meanwhile some Indians stood on the shore, yelling and motioning to them to come to land lest they be capsized. But they were quick to decide between two perils: that of the waters and that of the Indians, who, they felt sure, were waiting to rob and murder them. Being out of arrow range, they had nothing to fear from the Indians while they remained afloat. But "Had we wished for a shot," says Jim, evidently priding himself on his self-restraint, "they were quite within rifle distance."

It was not long, however, before they learned that the Indians had had excellent reasons to warn them against the waters.

Late in the evening, with landsmen's ignorance of the ocean and its tides, they lashed their canoes to some small trees and pitched their tents on a low-lying point of land. Sylvester took the first watch, while the others lay down to sleep. It was not long before, hearing a rushing sound and thinking a storm of wind and rain to be approaching, he roused his followers so that they might prepare their blankets, which they stretched out above them to keep out the water. This action, they soon realized, was about as useful as to raise an umbrella to keep the mud off one's feet. The supposed storm was really a tide, which rose in a ridge "like water over a milldam." Within twenty minutes three feet of water covered the men's sleeping place; their blankets were floating on the current; and they were in the canoes, which with difficulty they prevented from capsizing.

Not knowing that the tide would fall again within a few hours, and fearing that the Indians would attack and kill them in their present unstrategic location, they passed an unenviable night. But the morning's bright sun restored much of their confidence; and, still believing that there were Spanish settlements farther along the river, they continued downstream with the descending tide, until after a few days the torrents from the sea threatened to inundate them.

Now, says Jim, with notable understatement, the party was "placed in a new position, not the least disheartening or trying, among the painful predicaments, in which fortune had placed us." Actually the wanderers were trapped, unable to make progress against the tides from below or the river current from above. At last they realized, in a bitter awakening, that the Spanish towns were as mythical as fabled Cibola; the only inhabitants of the country were the savages, whose bloody intentions they had reason to suspect.

Their dismay was all the deeper since they carried a small fortune in furs—enough, asserts Jim, to constitute "a little independence for each one of us." But in a moment of clear-seeing he asks, "In this predicament, what were furs to us?" Their natural impulse was to throw all this useless baggage into the river. But on second thought they decided to go back upstream as far as possible and bury the furs before starting away on foot. They well knew that, in a desolate land which provided little in the way of subsistence, the odds were heavily against them—all the more so in view of the danger of Indian attack. Jim's ideas about the Indians—ideas that took no account at all of the kindly treatment received from some of them, such as the Navahos and the Cocopas—are contained in his statement that the land was "full of Indians who are to the last degree savage and murderous, and whom nothing can subdue to kindness and friendship."

Resolved to die rather than put themselves in the power of the red men, the wanderers made slow progress upstream, moving with the tide whenever it ascended, and subsequently—when the tide had ceased to flow—propelling themselves by means of poles and a towing rope, which must have required extreme exertion. But after some days it was clear that further efforts would be useless, and that the time had come to bury the furs. Nothing now remained except to push overland to the coast of California. Even at this crisis, a certain optimism remained to drive the men on, for they thought—on the basis of Indian reports—that the coast could not be far away.

Six days passed before they buried the last fur. And then began the long, hard, perilous trek to an unknown fate in unknown territory. Each man carried a pack that contained two blankets, a supply of dried beaver meat, a rifle, and ammunition. Unused to walking, since most of their travels had been accomplished on horseback or muleback, the men were soon complaining of stiff, sore limbs—the more so as they had to traverse a difficult country of scrubby brush and tall grass and vines. But as yet, though they may not have realized it, they were comparatively fortunate. For they still had water.

After a day or two they reached a barren plain which paralleled the river, and set out to the northwest across this salty waste. The narrator does not say why they chose this unpromising route, but probably they assumed it was the quickest way to the coast—and perhaps all other routes looked equally forbidding. The region, however, was truly an inferno. Though the month was February, the desert sun was so hot that it seemed "as if the heavens and earth were on fire." The dry, sandy soil, into which they sank up to the ankles, impeded their progress; their tongues became parched, they suffered agonies of thirst, and nowhere was there a drop of moisture. But why had they taken no water bags with them? Perhaps they had not realized the dire necessity, or perhaps they were already burdened with all the weight they could carry. Yet surely some of the buried beaver skins could have been fashioned into containers for the precious moisture.

Next day, with little thought in their minds except of water, they resumed the weary pilgrimage. Until early afternoon they kept on, and then in enormous relief they saw a small lake. They rushed down to drink—and how the imps of the desert must have mocked! The water was salt! It would only add to their thirst! And there was no inlet or other watercourse in sight!

After making rafts out of dry flags as a means of carrying their packs, they swam the lake. They might reasonably have expected to find fresh water on the farther shore, which was timbered, but they looked in vain for the precious substance. However, they drew some hope from observing the fresh footprints of Indians, which they took to mean that drinking water was obtainable near at hand. With the idea of locating an Indian encampment—despite what he says about the "savage and murderous" Indians, and the impossibility of moving them by kindness or friendship—Jim and a comrade climbed a hill, from whose summit they observed some smoke about ten miles to the south. This sight, he reports, gave them "great courage and hope," for surely there was water somewhere not far off. Filled with new animation, the company pushed on and after a time reached a rise from which they looked down on forty or fifty Indians, including women and children.

At this point there is an apparent inconsistency in the narrative. Jim tells us that it was about two in the afternoon when they came upon the lake, and later says it was about

three when they saw the Indians. Considering that the Indians
were some ten miles from the first point of observation, this
would involve an impossible speed for any pedestrian. But it
may be that the Indians they saw were not the ones responsible
for the smoke. And details of time and distance are, after
all, of minor importance. One can hardly suppose that Jim,
composing his diary more than two years after the events,
could have precisely recalled the hour at which every incident
occurred, even though his memory may have been accurate
as to more essential matters.

Having observed the Indians, the men had to make a
decision. Two plans were possible: "the long and uncertain
course of conciliation," and the much more daring and risky
but much speedier expedient of rushing down among the
natives and boldly asking for water. However, it was not their
reason that made the decision; it was their thirst, which for-
bade patience. Having examined their arms, so as to be sure
that these would be ready in case of need, the men boldly made
the move that might bring them to their trail's end beneath a
volley of arrows, or else might give them the boon they craved
above all other things on earth.

9

Desert Passage

As THE eight worn and desperate wanderers bore down upon the native encampment, the Indians reacted about as modern townsmen might do if a pack of famished wolves were suddenly let loose among them. But the newcomers did not try to check the flight of the Indians; their one thought still was water, which they found in more than sufficient quantity, and bent down to drink with a mad eagerness. Sylvester, who alone of all the party kept his wits, cautioned his followers that it would be dangerous to drink too much. But the others heeded him not at all and soon became deathly sick from so suddenly filling their parched stomachs.

Meanwhile Sylvester, schooled in the ways of the Indians, warned that the warriors would return after hiding their women and children. Hardly had he spoken when his words came true. Painted black and screaming like devils, the red men rushed forth with their clubs, their bows and arrows; while the whites, grouped together behind a fallen tree, prepared to fire if necessary. But in response to signs the Indians halted and ceased their commotion, apparently consulting one another in perplexity. Meanwhile the strangers made further signs, in an effort to convey an idea of their friendliness. Then to their delight they heard a voice in Spanish. "Who are you?"

"Americans!" they called back. And the Indian echoed this word. "Americans?" He then asked, Were they Christians? Were they friendly? Would they make a treaty? To all this, of course, the whites shouted back an eager "Yes!"

Eight Indians then came forward to carry on the discussions, while the others, their weapons poised for action, kept at a safe distance. After the negotiators had taken seats on the ground, the Patties learned that the Spanish-speaking Indian had been at Santa Catalina Mission in the Mexican province of California, from which he had escaped after being threatened with punishment for some minor offense. The interpreter now transmitted some obvious questions. Who were the whites? How had they come to this place? And why? And what adventures had they met? Having received satisfactory answers and smoked the pipe of peace, the Indians buried the war ax in a hole in the ground; and with it, according to their picturesque belief, they buried all animosity.

They now asked if their other men might come and talk to the whites, who, after some discussion, agreed on condition that they come unarmed. The Indians then asked their visitors to stay with them for three or four days, so that they might meet the head chief, who was encamped two days' journey to the south. Exhausted as they were and deeply in need of rest, Sylvester and his men could have found no invitation more to their liking.

The women and children, who at first were very shy, were now brought near. Like the members of other desert tribes, they wore no clothes; and they were understandably curious about their strange visitors, who displayed bright red cotton cloths on their chests and hid their limbs behind queer wrappings. What chiefly interested the Indians was what lay beneath the clothes: they admired, says Jim, the "red flannel shirts, and the white skin *under them;* for little show of whiteness was to be seen in our faces." Losing their bashfulness, they opened the white men's shirts to examine the skin beneath, and were amazed to find how much softer it was than their own. And then, doubtless wishing to discover whether white men were built like other men, they motioned to a particularly fair-skinned member of the party, indicating that they wanted him to strip himself in order to appease their curiosity. At first he refused, but later, after they had brought him a gift of some dried fish, he yielded to their entreaties and the persuasions of his comrades. And after he had complied, they remained talking among themselves and laughing and stood near him to compare his body with theirs. But their good will had been won, and all during the stay of the white men they brought feasts of cooked fish, vegetables, and roots.

Within a few days the head chief arrived—a serious looking man of about fifty, his hair tinged with gray. Having put some questions, which the whites answered to his satisfaction, he was told that his visitors were eager to reach the white settlements and there buy horses to bring them back to their own country. If he would supply guides to take them to the white settlements, they would pay him well.

What would they give him? was the natural response. And so they showed him some excellent currency: their blankets. The chief professed himself to be pleased, but admitted that he would have been even better pleased with another form of currency: some red cloth.

Eager to be obliging, the white men stripped off their shirts and tore them into ribbons, which were eagerly received by

the people, who tied them joyously about their heads and
limbs. In such a warm climate, after all, shirts were of no
value to the men. And as for blankets—they would be only a
burden to carry. Two of these were presented to the chief;
and everybody, accordingly, was well satisfied. The chief, in
order to make good his part of the bargain, designated two
guides to accompany the white men to the Mexican settlements, and the whites agreed to pay these guides upon reaching their destination.

All now was moving forward beautifully. The party seemed
to have gone far toward extracting itself from its dire predicament of a few days before. Piloted by the two Indians, the
men should have little difficulty in reaching the Mexican
habitations—and after that all would be well. So, at least, they
may have persuaded themselves. How little they could foresee
the coming ordeal!

Neither of the guides, unfortunately, spoke Spanish. And
so their charges followed them in silence as they started off
toward a snowy mountain to the southwest. We are not told
what time of day it was, but the guides indicated by means of
signs that they should reach the foot of the mountain by midnight—a feat which appeared impossible to the Patties. Worn
as they were and untrained to the rigors of desert trails, how
could they keep up with Indians who had passed their lives
in this wilderness? By the time they had reached the summit
of a high, steep hill, they were thirsty and extremely tired. But
they had no water; they could see only the vast sweep of the
salty plain stretching between them and the snow mountain;
and they were so afraid of receiving disheartening information
that they did not ask the guide if any water might be found
between them and the mountain.

Even on horseback the trip would have been difficult. But
to the pedestrians plodding along with their guns and provisions, fatigued almost to the point of exhaustion and thirst-

ing to the point of agony, that bout with the desert was the most purgatorial of all their experiences. Not a cloud interfered with the blazing brilliance of the sun, which warmed the sand, in which they floundered up to the ankles, until Jim thought it "almost hot enough to roast eggs in." The air was bone dry. A single scrubby tree, in the course of the day, lent them a momentary shade. But when they lay down for a few minutes' badly needed rest, the Indians motioned them to be on their way and made them understand that they would find no water before reaching the mountains. They now began to fear that they never would reach the mountains.

In their desperate effort to extract a little moisture, they tried to chew tobacco; they even rolled bullets about in their mouths; and in their extremity they resorted to other expedients of the most revolting nature, such as to drink their own urine. But nothing having proved of any use, two of the party surrendered in utter exhaustion and lay down in the shade of a bush. "Their tongues," relates Jim, "were so swollen, and their eyes so sunk in their head, that they were a spectacle to behold." None of the others expected to see them again, and they themselves had probably given up hope.

But the remaining six still struggled on and on toward the mountain, which still appeared far away. By this time a paralysis seemed to have overcome their wills, so that they moved like automatons. And all the while, as if to add to their difficulties, the dazzle of the sun so reflected itself in the white sands that they were scarcely able to see their way.

The guides, who bore the heat and dryness "like camels in the Arabian desert," did their best to motion the straggling men forward, unavailingly urging them to greater speed. And somehow the six did keep on their way until nightfall, when they had relief from the sun's torrid blaze. It was now too dark to go on even if they had had the strength.

Therefore they made a large fire, though we are left to

wonder what fuel the desert supplied, which could be gathered by men in their exhausted state. By the light of the bonfire, they hoped, the two comrades whom they had left behind might be able to determine where they were and rejoin them. As an additional summons, they fired some guns, which were answered by distant shots, and continued to fire at intervals, while the two stragglers approached and eventually were reunited with their friends.

The reunion, however, was not a joyous one. The two men, disappointed and angry, asked why they had not been left to die in peace. For they had interpreted the rifle shots as signals reporting the finding of water.

One of the pair, apparently in the hope of putting an end to his sufferings, then drew out a small phial of laudanum and swallowed the contents. But instead of killing him, it produced an unnatural exhilaration and caused him to talk and laugh gaily and to feel whole and well again, just as if he were not thirsting to death in the heart of the desert.

The others meanwhile scraped under the sand to a depth at which it was a little cool, and lay down, after completely undressing. But the Indians, who stretched themselves out near by, covered themselves with their blankets. It is eloquent of the white men's suspicion of the Indians that Sylvester asked Jim to lie on the edge of one of these blankets, so that the guides should not run off in the night, leaving the white men to certain death. But apparently the guides had no such treacherous intention.

In the morning, reinvigorated by the coolness of the night and by a good sleep, the party started off with fresh energy. But their greatest trial lay just ahead. By mid-morning they had reached the foot of "a sand hill about half a mile in height, and very steep." The worst feature of all was that the sand, being loose, gave little foothold, causing the travelers to slip back in their steps and swiftly exhausting them. Complicating this ghastly situation was the fact that the sun now beamed down with the same intolerable heat as yesterday, so that the air seemed to "scald" the sufferers' lungs. The original route up the hill having proved impossible, the men turned north to a point at which the ascent was not so steep, and sometime in the afternoon part of the company laboriously reached the summit. But only part!

For two members of the group the climb had been too much. Sylvester and a comrade named Slover, both of them far beyond the usual age of pathfinders, were overcome by the heat, the glare, the thirst, and the back-breaking exertions. In their exhausted state they had given up hope and had thrown themselves down on the burning earth to die.

Jim's plight may be imagined. He did not wish to leave his father to perish alone there in the desert; yet to remain would mean certain death for himself as well. Nevertheless he chose to remain. But Sylvester, weak as he was, had strength enough to protest even amid his torment. Jim must go with the others; in that way, and that way only, he might save Sylvester also. For if he came upon water, he might return with his powder horn full. Otherwise, he himself would die without having in any way helped his father.

To this logic Jim bowed. Leaving Sylvester and Slover, he plodded painfully on to the top of the hill, where the five other whites and the two Indians awaited him. He says nothing at all of his feelings, except that he and the others had satisfied their consciences that they had taken the right course. But the impulse to live still burned strong within them, pushing them on, urging them to struggle down the hill, and then up another sandy eminence. And well for them that they persisted! From the top of the second hill they saw a sight that was worth more to them than all the fabled wealth of Eldorado. The sequel is best told in Jim's own words:

The Eternal Power, who hears the ravens when they cry . . . had had mercy upon us! Imagine my joy at seeing a clear, beautiful running stream of water, just below us at the foot of the hill! Such a blissful sight I had never seen before, and never expect to see again.

Having run down the hill, they repeated their folly of some days before, when they had come upon water at the Indian encampment. Instead of sipping cautiously, they drank their fill of the cold product of the melted snows; and their stomachs, unable to endure the intake after the long drought, rebelled and caused them acute pain and vomiting.

Though sick like the others, Jim thought of his father and Slover, lying exhausted and near to death on the blazing hillside. He therefore emptied his power horn and filled it with water. Then, along with a companion, who likewise carried a powder horn full of the priceless liquid, he hastened back to the stranded pair.

The two men were stretched out as before on the broiling sand, fast asleep beneath a fiery, cloudless sky. At first Jim had a great shock, for as the sufferers lay there supine, motionless and with sunken eyes, his impression was that they were dead. In alarm he ran to his father; but Sylvester, along with Slover, immediately awakened and drank the water.

This so revived them that in less than an hour they were able to climb the hill, and before dark they had reached the remainder of the party, who were encamped by the stream. A great fire had been lighted; and all, just as if they had not touched shoulders with death himself and escaped by the width of an eyelid, were now in the gayest of spirits. The Indians, singing and dancing, seemed to be giving thanks to the Great Spirit. And the white men, roasting some of their beaver meat and taking food for the first time in forty-eight hours, appeared to share in the feelings of the natives. One of the party, a German immigrant, expressed the general feeling in his quaint, broken English. The desert over which they had just passed, he insisted, "should be named the devil's plain, for . . . it was more hotter as hell, and none but teyvils could live upon it." During the passage of the wasteland, Jim adds, they had seen "not a single bird, nor the track of any quadruped, or in fact any thing that had life, nor even a spring, wood or grass blade, except a single scrubby tree, under which we found a little shade."

What he evidently means is that they had found only one kind of tree, for he mentions the "prickly pears" as sometimes existing in such abundance as to puzzle them how to find a path between the thorns (apparently he is referring to some form of cactus, whose name he seemed not to know).

One wishes that it were possible to pinpoint his route, but this cannot be done on the basis of his descriptions. However, it is obvious that the Patties were somewhere in the Colorado Desert, that hot, low-lying wasteland which runs a hundred and fifty or two hundred miles north and south from the Gulf of California to the San Bernardino Mountains. The general course of the party, from the lower Colorado River to San Diego, makes it certain that the worst of their trials were endured in the southern Colorado Desert; and this is confirmed by Jim's statement that "the Sahara of California runs north and south, and is bounded on each side by high barren mountains, some of which are covered by perpetual snow."

This correctly describes the Colorado Desert, which extends on the west to the tall San Jacinto range and on the east is bordered by the Chocolate Mountains, which run southeast to the Colorado River. Jim did not know, of course, of the much larger Mohave Desert, which might more properly be called "the Sahara of California." Nor could he or any of his comrades have foreseen the changes that were to transform certain parts of the territory—perhaps even parts that they had traversed—when the miracle of irrigation would cause the

once-barren Coachella and Imperial valleys to put forth flowers
and green leafage, a luxuriance of vines and orchards, of date
groves, and of cotton and alfalfa fields.

With the finding of the life-giving stream, the travelers'
troubles may have seemed to be over—they could not have
known of the severe trials still ahead. For a while, however, all
went well. They journeyed through a land of palm trees and
live oaks, a welcome contrast to the sparsely vegetated desert;
they killed a deer, to the delight of the Indian guides; and after
about a week they met some converted Indians from Santa
Catalina Mission, in Lower California, and received from
them the welcome information that they were only four days
from this mission. They therefore released their guides, each
of whom they rewarded with a blanket; and while these men
left to rejoin their own people, the whites resumed the journey
with the aid of new Indian guides. And now, as they climbed
the coastal range, their difficulties began anew.

The mountains were so tall and steep that they had to toil
for two days and a half to reach the top. Even for hikers armed
with the toughest modern equipment, the climb would be
arduous; but to the eight weary wanderers, who had nothing
but thin deerskin moccasins to protect them from the sharp
rocks that covered most of the trail, the ascent could only
have been a long ordeal. For Jim this ordeal was even more
painful than for the others, as an injury to his heel forced him
to hobble in extreme torment. He kept on as long as he could,
but finally the wound brought on a fever, and the inflamed and
swollen member refused any further service. With a rock for
couch, he lay down and told his comrades that he could not
go on until he felt better.

The others, and particularly his father, urged him to push
forward; the mission, they said, was no more than three miles
away, and he should make an effort to reach it. But three miles
might have been three thousand, so far as his ability to walk

was concerned. Finally, therefore, Jim's comrades agreed to go to the mission for a horse with which to rescue him. Feeling severe chills, he lit a fire; while the Indians, before leaving him to himself, warned him under no condition to go to sleep, since the mountains abounded in grizzly bears, one of which might pick him for a meal.

Nevertheless, having examined his gun and pistol and found them in order, Jim did go to sleep. And when he was awakened it was not by a prowling bear but by two Indians from Santa Catalina, who told him that the corporal of the guard wished him to come to the mission. This, however, only angered Jim, who in his sickness and misery was by no means in the best of humors; but they assured him that the corporal wanted him at the mission only so that he would not be eaten by a grizzly. Why then, he asked, had the corporal not sent a horse for him? There was none available just then, answered the Indians, and therefore they had come to carry him.

It was a strange ride that he now took, mounted on the back of one of the men, while the other assisted by carrying his arms. These Indians must truly have had Herculean powers! But they did reach the mission with their human baggage, and there Jim was treated to a fresh surprise. After all their limb-wearying and heart-wrenching adventures; after bouts with savage Indians and the still more savage wilderness; after privation, thirst, wounds, and hunger; after the long, long trek which had brought them face to face with the leering skull of death, and which they had survived only by a miracle; after the hopes of many days, the dream of welcoming hands at the first Mexican settlement, the expectation of help in their effort to return to their own land—what reception had the travelers actually met? Something that in all their wild imaginings they had probably never visualized. They had been thrown into the guardhouse!

Naturally the victims were as indignant as they were

amazed. They showed their passport; but their jailors would not be convinced that they had not come with illegal and evil intentions. After all, how could they be sure of the identity, character, or purposes of these rough-looking, half-clad vagabonds, who, lacking even shirts, had popped up as if from nowhere, with a yarn of being American trappers whose horses had been stolen by the Indians, leaving them no choice but to cross the impassable desert to California? It is not difficult to see the Patties' story may have seemed incredible to the Mexican officials.

For a week the eight Americans were held in prison, while being fed but once a day on a sort of corn mush. The enforced inactivity, however, served at least one purpose: it gave Jim's wounded foot time to heal. We can imagine how relieved the captives were when the week was over and they were led away, even though under escort of a corps of soldiers. Despite his predicament, Jim could not help noticing the striking scenery: the high mountains, penetrated by beautiful streams, which surrounded the Mission of Santa Catalina; and the equally imposing mountains in addition to the magnificent ocean views from the Mission of St. Sebastian, which the party reached after two days. Around the mission, which supported (according to Jim) a population of about six hundred, there were rich orchards and vineyards, fields of grain, and a fair supply of cattle.

The prisoners were received by a swarthy sergeant, who greeted them politely and led them to the guardhouse, which he asked them to tolerate until he could make more suitable arrangements. Having been told that they were hungry, he had a tottering old steer killed, and served its flesh along with some corn, which reminded Jim of the arrangements made in Kentucky, "to prepare a mess for a diseased cow." They were not even permitted to eat this disgusting fare in peace or privacy; when it had been cooked, they were brought forth into the yard, while men, women, and children stood about to watch "as though they had been at a menagerie to see some wild and unknown animals." And indeed the ragged and emaciated wanderers may have looked as strange as animals in a menagerie.

Not being pleased to be regarded as exhibition pieces, they asked whether they should be taken for brutes rather than human beings; and there may have been insolence as well as anger in their voices, for they provoked an insolent reply, to the effect that they were not Christians and therefore were little better than animals. Continuing the wrathful interchange, the prisoners asserted that they were truer Christians than their captors; and they backed this claim with an effective argument. Incredibly, they had not been deprived of their guns, and they threatened to take these and hunt their own food. One instantly asks why, if they still had their guns, they had permitted themselves to be imprisoned at all, and Jim's explanation is only partly convincing: that they considered their captors to be mere subordinates who had exceeded their authority and who would be reversed as soon as the higher officials were informed of the facts—indeed, the victims expected not only to be set free but to receive compensation for their mistreatment. But if they had revolted—or so we may suppose them to have reasoned—they would have placed themselves under a shadow with the authorities.

Now that the prisoners had resolved to take matters into their own hands, their captors were alarmed. The sergeant returned, asked why they were displeased, examined their food, pronounced it unfit for a dog, promised to provide something more suitable, and duly had the prisoners served with mutton and tortillas, which were just what they wanted. Thus the incipient rebellion was put down.

They then asked the sergeant to intercede for them with his commanding officer, so that they might purchase horses and return to the United States. The sergeant replied that he would write to the governor, from whom an answer might be expected in about two weeks; he had no doubt that the request of the Americans would be granted. Meanwhile he allowed his eight charges freedom to hunt, to gather honey, and to roam the cliffs of the picturesque countryside, from which they gazed out over the sea at a great variety of creatures, including seals, sea otters, whales, sharks, and other aquatic monsters.

Eventually the governor's reply reached them, in the shape of a body of mounted soldiers, who were to convey the Americans to his headquarters in San Diego. They received this summons with delight, for they did not doubt that the official would recognize the merits of their case and grant their request. One would suppose, however, that they would have taken warning from the number of the soldiers—seventeen in all, including a corporal. Surely the governor would not have sent so many men on a mere routine mission to guard prisoners of no importance.

Permitted to ride from time to time when they became tired, they had not too difficult a journey. They traveled through a mountainous country where wild oats and clover grew luxuriantly; visited more than one mission, including that of St. Michael, located in the midst of orchards, vineyards, and planted fields; and passed through ranges where multitudes of horses and cattle browsed. And eventually they came in sight of the port of San Diego, where they were reminded of their own country by the ship *Franklin* of Boston.

They now had an intimation of what lay ahead. The corporal in charge of them here—it is not evident whether or not he was the one who had traveled with them from Santa Catalina Mission—now asked that they give up their arms. It was the rule, he explained, that all strangers must turn over their weapons to be deposited in the guardhouse. At first the Americans refused, maintaining that they were capable of carrying their own weapons to the guardhouse; but the corporal pleaded that he himself was responsible to the governor for the surrender of their arms. And as they did not wish to interfere with his performance of his duty, they acceded to his demand—with results that they were bitterly to regret. They did not think, says Jim, that this was the last time they would "have the pleasure of shouldering these trusty friends."

Greatly fatigued, they arrived at the guardhouse, on one side of which their arms were stacked. When they threw themselves down to sleep, no misgivings for the morrow troubled them; and the innumerable fleas, which dotted their bodies with small specks and put spots of blood all over the shirts that they had received at one of the missions, did little to impair their sanguine mood.

It was at eight in the morning, two days later, that they were ushered into the office of Governor José María de Echeandía and were subjected to the interview with which our story opened.

10

In the Guardhouse

As THE men were herded out of the office of Governor Echeandía, a fierce resolve flamed up in Sylvester's mind. "My
boys," he urged, "as soon as we arrive at the guardhouse, let
us seize our arms!" It would be a do-or-die attempt: now that
all their hopes had been punctured and nothing lay before
them but the prospect of imprisonment, what had they to
lose? They would either make good their escape or be shot
down while defending themselves like men—and even to be
shot down would be better than to stay here and be murdered
in cold blood.

The others at once agreed and walked back eagerly to the
guardhouse. But there their hopes were suddenly quenched.
Their arms—even down to the pocket knives that had been
removed on a search of their persons—had all disappeared. No
choice, therefore, remained except to yield and, worst of all,
to let themselves be placed in separate quarters—which, says
Jim, "seemed the death stroke to us all. Affection and mutual

suffering and danger had endeared us to each other, and this separation seemed like rending our hearts."

Overcome by emotion, Jim threw his arms about his father, burst into tears, and, as if struck by a grisly premonition, cried out that he "foresaw that the parting would be forever." Sylvester reproved him for this outburst, which he called weak and unmanly; yet he, too, seemed overcome by his own bleak thoughts.

A ray of hope came when the sergeant, noting Jim's grief and being told that Sylvester was his father, volunteered to inform the governor of their relationship, in the belief that Echeandía would permit the two to be lodged together. Now for a time, when the sergeant had left to see the governor, Jim was in "an agony of suspense." But this suspense was to be short-lived. The sergeant, upon his return, stated that Echeandía had been angered at the request to confine two prisoners in one cell; the original instructions were to be followed. Seeing some soldiers who had been sent to lock the prisoners in their cages, Jim and his comrades embraced one another, and each went to meet his separate fate.

Though he declares that "I will say nothing of my feelings," he really does say quite a little, and goes so far as to remark that he had no desire to live except "to sustain the increasing age and infirmities of my father." He also conveys a good idea of how he felt in his prison, a windowless den eight or ten feet square, with a door marked by iron crossbars, through which he could look out on a dim aisle. Over the outer door there was a sign, in capitals: DESTINACIÓN DE LA CATTIVO. On the stone floor Jim's blanket had been placed as a couch. All hope seems to have been quenched in the captive as he entered this dreary dungeon, which he looked upon with extreme pessimism as his "everlasting abode." One of his most expressive passages follows:

Liberty is dear to every one, but doubly dear to one, who had from infancy been accustomed to free range, and to be guided by his own will. Put a man, who has ranged the prairies, and exulted in the wilderness, as I have for years, in a prison, to let him have a full taste of the blessings of freedom, and the horror of shackles and confinement! I passed the remainder of the day in fierce walking backwards and forwards, over my stone floor, with no object to contemplate, but my swarthy sentinel, through the grate.

At this point his imagination may have asserted itself, as was only natural in one so cruelly and undeservedly confined. He reports that the sergeant "seemed to be true to his office, and fitly selected for his business, for I thought I saw him look at me through the grate with the natural exultation and joy of a bad heart in the view of misery."

It is probable that the prisoner was developing a persecution complex and saw malice in the mere ordinary thoughtless routine of the guardhouse. It is thus that captured men have always looked upon the instruments of their captivity.

Night brought a darkness that was "the darkness of the grave." But it came with no blessed dreams. While the victim tossed on his blanket on the stone floor, he visited his father in imagination and pictured for himself his condition and state of mind. And at times his thoughts ranged to the future, trying to fathom the fate that awaited his comrades and himself. But amid all his fevered ruminations he was denied the blessing, the escape, of sleep.

In the dim light of morning he could see the governor's office across the aisle from his cell, and in the door the governor himself was standing. The frenzy of Jim's feelings literally cries out in his next utterance: "Ah! that I had but my trusty rifle well charged to my face! Could I have had the pleasure of that single shot, I think I would have been willing to have purchased it with my life."

But wishes, as he says, "are not rifle balls"—a fact for which he should have been devoutly grateful.

At eight o'clock the church bells tolled, a drum rolled, and a soldier brought Jim his breakfast, which consisted of about a pint of beans and corn cooked in rancid tallow. One whiff was enough. In the evening when the soldier returned with more of the same rations, the foul mess was still untasted; but the soldier, upon hearing Jim's complaints, flung the whole concoction into his face, saying it was good enough for a brute. Jim reciprocated the compliment, and the soldier left in a fury, to be seen no more that night. But even had the food been good, the prisoner could not have eaten. For he was becoming sick.

Not everyone, however, was to treat him unkindly. The sergeant, visiting him, asked about his health; put some friendly questions about his past, his adventures, and his family; and procured him two good and well-cooked dishes, which he refused to eat until assured that his comrades were equally well fed. Jim meanwhile tried in vain to drag forth some information about Sylvester, whom the sergeant had seen but had been unable to converse with.

Next day the sergeant again brought Jim's dinner, but his prisoner was too sick to eat. And in the evening he came with supper, along with a very pleasant surprise in the form of another visitor, his sister. We here find one of those gaps that occur so frequently in the *Personal Narrative*. Jim describes the girl only vaguely as "a young lady of great personal beauty," and does not even mention her name at this point, though many pages later we read of her as "Miss Peak" (which may have been his rendering of the Spanish "Pico").

In any case, we are given to understand that the sergeant's sister took a real interest in Jim and asked him many questions, including his age and the circumstances that had taken him so far from his own country. When she left, she promised to pray for him, and—doubtless more to his liking—said that she would speak to the governor on his behalf and do everything she could to alleviate his lot while he remained in prison. He adds that, due to "the ministrations of a kind spirit," his sleep that night was "sound and dreamless."

Her intercession with Echeandía, as he might have foreseen, was insufficient to bring the boon he most desired—liberty. But it did have some effect, for he was granted a bed and a change of clothing, and thenceforth had no complaints as to food and drink. Besides, the girl's visits were often repeated—bright spots amid the general darkness.

Meanwhile, Jim made another acquaintance—Captain John Bradshaw, of the United States vessel *Franklin*, which the prisoners, upon their arrival, had seen in the harbor of San Diego. As depicted in other accounts, Bradshaw was little more than a notorious smuggler; yet it was not in this light that Jim saw him, but rather as "a true hearted American," who, "fearless of danger and consequences," came to see Jim without leave after being denied permission by the governor.

But apparently the captain had motives even apart from sympathy for an imprisoned fellow countryman. The discussion having turned to the subject of the buried furs, the captain asked about the possibility of rescuing them and went on to inquire whether Jim and his comrades would try to recover them if they had the chance, and whether, if they did regain the furs, they would sell them to Bradshaw. Jim, of course, could not answer for the others, but he was not alone in being asked these questions: Bradshaw successively visited each of the eight prisoners, with precisely the same queries, and from each of the eight he received a ready "Yes!" Why, indeed, should the men not accede to anything at all that he asked? Had he not promised to make every effort to obtain their release?

Having tried in vain to move the hard-headed Echeandía

by pretenses of friendship, Bradshaw resorted to what Jim calls "an innocent stratagem." Claiming to need an interpreter in order to do business with a Mexican merchant, he mentioned having heard that one of the American prisoners spoke Spanish fluently. If, therefore, the governor would let the prisoner out of the guardhouse for a few hours, the captain would give his bond in any amount for the captive's return. Somewhat surprisingly, considering that he had steadfastly refused most other petitions, Echeandía consented. And Jim had the great joy of seeing his cell door swing open.

If the governor had sent spies to follow Jim during his period out of jail (and perhaps he did), he would not have observed any dealings with a Mexican merchant. He would have seen that the released man, along with Bradshaw and his supercargo Rufus Perkins, visited the captain in charge of the arms, assured him of the integrity and good purposes of all the American prisoners, and induced him to use his influence with the governor in order to obtain permission for the prisoners to go after their buried furs. During the half-hour in which the Spanish captain of arms was absent for an interview with Echeandía, Jim was able to speak to his father, though separated by a barred door, and was told that he too had been visited by the beautiful young Miss Peak, the sergeant's sister, who had ministered with great kindness to him and all his comrades. Jim likewise stole a few words with each of the other prisoners, to the delight of them all.

Back in the office of the captain of arms, Jim heard the results of the latest appeal to the governor. That official, as on most occasions, had proved immovable; the request had been refused. However, Echeandía had professed a desire to see some papers Jim had spoken of, signed by the President of the United States and testifying that the Patties and their friends were in truth Americans. Jim, returning to his cell "less buoyant and more completely desponding" than ever, apparently saw no hope in this latest maneuver; and his pessimism was confirmed when in a little while Bradshaw and Perkins came to him with the word that Echeandía was unmoved by Jim's papers. While speaking to him through the cell door, the visitors were interrupted by the guard, who ordered them to leave and stated that the governor had forbidden them ever to speak with Jim again.

Doubtless this command, heartless as it may seem, was justified in Echeandía's mind by the knowledge that Jim, having gained his temporary release in order to serve as interpreter for Bradshaw, had actually spent his time in unauthorized pursuits, even paying forbidden visits to his father and the other Americans. Toward Bradshaw and Perkins, since the former's "innocent stratagem" may not have seemed innocent from an official point of view, Echeandía's feelings may not have been much more friendly than toward the other Americans.

For Jim a black interval ensued—even blacker than the grim preceding period. His only relief, for two weeks, was in the visits of the young lady, though the governor had ordered these calls to be "few and far between." Then one day the sergeant brought him a note from his father. It was a note such as few could have read dry-eyed. For paper Sylvester had used a bit of cardboard from his hat. For pen he had employed a stick, and for ink he had drawn the blood from his veins. The letters were difficult to make out, and the import of the message was that Sylvester was sick beyond hope of recovery and had but one wish before he died: to see his son again. He therefore urged Jim to make every effort to obtain permission to visit him, but if this permission were not granted, Jim would still know that his father's love was with him.

"This letter," says Jim, "pierced me to the heart. O, could I have flown through my prison walls! Had I possessed the strength of the giants, how soon would I have levelled them, even had I drawn down destruction on my own head." But he had not the strength of giants, and there was nothing, nothing he could do to pierce the walls or to cover the few yards to the cell where his father lay mortally ill. He did, to be sure, beg the sergeant to intercede with the governor; but the sergeant, returning with face downcast, revealed the bitter results even before his faltering voice had stammered out the facts.

Well might Jim exclaim, "Oh God! of what stuff are some hearts made!" Yet it is probable that the governor, who had been imposed upon by various Americans, was blinded by his own suspicions and unable to see that this latest request was bona fide, and not the result of a ruse whereby two contemptible foreigners planned to confer and hatch a plot against the authorities.

Only slightly consoled by the sergeant's promise that Sylvester would lack no food or help that he could bring him, Jim passed a miserable night. In the morning he received some comfort from a visit from Miss Peak, whose tear-brimmed eyes expressed her sympathy. But nothing could bring him any real solace; his grief was such that he could hardly eat, and during the succeeding days he became so emaciated that he had scarcely the strength to walk the length of his cell.

Then, on the twenty-fourth of April, just four weeks after their first interview with Echeandía, the sergeant came to Jim with the dread, expected news.

At this, Jim confessed, he "felt relieved." His father had been "set free"—set free from cruelty and oppression and from a life that, ever since his wife's death, had been a burden to him. Jim himself, weak and exhausted, expected to join him in a few days. For him, too, he adds, life was a burden and one of which he "longed to be relieved."

At night Señorita Peak once more visited Jim with her unfailing evidences of sympathy and brought him a suit of black in which to attend the funeral. Jim pointed out, however, that the prison walls still enclosed him; and to this the girl replied that she had pleaded with the governor and obtained his permission for Jim to be let out on this solemn occasion. Doubtless they both reflected upon the biting irony of the fact that, not having been released to see his father when the latter was still alive, Jim was granted this boon when Sylvester lay cold and lifelesss.

Under a glaring sky, beneath which he reeled, a file of soldiers led the bereaved man to the grave. No prayers were said as the black coffin was lowered; an unceremonious haste marked the dropping of the earth upon the wooden lid. In tears, the sergeant's sister accompanied Jim back to his cell door, but his own lids were dry; the tears somehow would not come. Upon reaching the prison, he was so revolted at the idea of re-entering the vile den that, he says, he would rather have been shot than have gone back. His one consolation was the thought that his own health was declining and that he would soon be at rest beside his father.

11

Prisoner's Progress

Jɪᴍ ᴍɪɢʜᴛ decide that he had reached a dead end, from which his life could not go on, but some deeper power within him would not accept the decree. The strength of the life force and the resiliency of his youth joined to proclaim that he must not, he would not end his existence in his miserable cell.

Somehow after a time sleep returned to him. Somehow his appetite revived, and with it his strength. He had the urge to resume his old habit of smoking and, having obtained some cigars from the sergeant, was soothed not only by the tobacco itself but by the pleasure of watching the smoke rings, which— in the absence of companions to speak to or of books to read— helped him to fill the interminable hours.

Two months went by. Then two events occurred, both of which were to cast their reflections on his life. The first may have been connected with Captain Bradshaw, whose vessel, the *Franklin*, had been seized on a charge of smuggling. The *Personal Narrative* does not give the details, but in Bancroft's

History of California (Volume III), we read that Bradshaw, having been "granted all possible privileges," was accused of a number of derelictions, "of having illegally transferred the cargo of another vessel to his own; of having touched at Santa Catalina in defiance of special orders; of having refused to show his invoices or make a declaration; and of insolence to the governor." Beyond this, Bradshaw and his supercargo Perkins, "being on shore, promised obedience to the order; but asked permission to go on board to make the necessary preparations, and when they refused to leave the vessel, laughed in the face of the Californians sent to convey and enforce—so far as possible by threats—Echeandía's order, and on July 11th changed anchorage to a point near the entrance of the harbor."

Under these circumstances the governor had more of a case than one would gather from Pattie's account.

Whether at Bradshaw's instigation or not, Jim received five ounces of gold from the captains and supercargoes of three other United States vessels, which chanced to be in the harbor; these are the captains whose names he mentions as Seth Rogers, Aaron W. Williams, and H. Cunningham. He goes on to say that they counseled him to hide the money from the Mexicans and hold it to use for his comrades and himself in case of emergency. Much about this incident, however, remains mysterious: why the captains should have felt such concern for Jim and his comrades, how they had managed to smuggle the gold in to him without arousing the suspicion of the guards, and how and where he contrived to secrete it.

At about the same time Jim was called to the governor's office and shown several packages of letters in English, which Echeandía could not translate owing to his ignorance of the language. No regular translator being available just then, the official asked Jim if he could read them; and being answered in the affirmative, he thrust a letter before him and asked him to translate it. This Jim did to Echeandía's satisfaction; and the governor, showing some interest in Jim, thereupon asked some questions about his travels, the length of his absence from his own country, and other personal matters. Upon dismissing him for the day, he remarked that he would probably ask for his services again.

He actually did call for him on several successive days, on each of which he received him with formal courtesy; while the translator, when he found his superior in a sufficiently good humor, would refer to his imprisonment and ask why the governor continued to treat innocent men as spies. Echeandía, with the dexterity of a skilled diplomat, would try to evade the issue, would protest that he would not willingly punish anyone unjustly, and that he would gladly release the prisoners if they could produce any "substantial proof" that they were not spies. Meanwhile Jim, though for a time he managed to keep down his anger, felt surer that every word spoken by the governor was "a vile and deceitful lie." But evidently he did not realize that he and Echeandía had been reared under the influence of two widely different systems of law: on the one hand, the Anglo-Saxon, which assumes a man to be innocent until he is proved guilty; and on the other hand, the Latin, which recognizes no such presumption of innocence and may put the burden of proof on an accused man to establish that he is not guilty. For men trained in such antagonistic traditions, no meeting of minds was likely; what would seem only right and natural to the one would strike the other as baseness and treachery.

Having made no progress toward the dismissal of the charges against the other Americans and himself, Jim now tried for success in a more limited field. Could Echeandía not let him and his comrades go out to recover the buried furs? Apparently Echeandía replied by expressing doubts (well-grounded doubts, one may be sure) that the men would ever return; but Jim met this argument by suggesting that some soldiers be sent to guard them, and by offering to pay for the soldiers and all other expenses. The governor listened noncommitally and promised to think the matter over and let Jim know his decision within a week. He then sent the prisoner back to his cell.

Jim thought he had now obtained a glimpse into Echeandía's character, and concluded that "like most arbitrary and cruel men, he was fickle and infirm of purpose." He therefore "determined to take advantage of that weakness in his character by seeming submissive to his wishes," while using all opportunities to plead for his liberty and for permission to go for the furs. Just how well he adhered to this resolution will soon be evident.

Four days later he was again summoned before the governor, for whom he had translated some letters relating to Captain Bradshaw and the detention of his ship and cargo. But when he asked whether Echeandía had reached any decision about the furs, his answer was a surly "No!" Jim's thoughts, as he went back to his cell, were equally surly. "How earnestly," he says, "I wished that he and I had been together in the wild woods, and I armed with my rifle!"

Now, quite forgetting his determination to "seem submissive" to Echeandía's wishes, he decided to do no more translating. Submissiveness, after all, was not a part of his disposition and in no way conformed to his wild and independent habit of life. Nor was prudence natural to him, and least of all the prudence of the diplomat; his surging emotions would not be put down by any considerations of cool, reasoned policy.

In serving the governor, Jim told himself, he was getting nowhere. Unfortunately he could not see through the murk of his own passions and realize that, by gradually worming his way into Echeandía's good will, he might in time have broken down the man's prejudices and hostility and even have gained his confidence, and with it the goals closest to his own heart.

But this would have required patience, restraint, wisdom, the clamping of a lid over the rebellious furies storming within him. Instead, pride, resentment, and rage took command, making Jim look forward to the opportunity of defying the enemy to his face.

That opportunity was no more than three days in coming. Called back to Echeandía's office, he took the proffered seat, while the governor turned to him with a smile and handed him a bundle of letters with a request that he translate them. Casually Jim opened one, glanced at it, then returned the bundle, arose, and blandly asked to go back to his prison.

The governor was presumably stunned. His glance resembled "that of an enraged wild beast"; his voice had a growl as he demanded to know why Jim would not do the translating. Jim's voice was equally gruff as he replied that he would not work for his oppressor, he would be no one's slave. At this the argument passed beyond words. Echeandía's tall form lunged forward; striking with the flat of his sword, he dealt Jim a blow that almost felled him. Then he called to his soldiers to fling Jim back to his cell, where he "should lay and rot." Jim, still not subdued, recovered from the blow on the head only to spring at the governor; but the guards seized him as he attempted this mad act, and started dragging him away.

Meanwhile Echeandía stood by, cursing. And Jim, even now not repressed, threw a taunting question: did it become an officer and a gentleman to beat an unarmed prisoner? If he only had a sword, he could kill many dastards such as the governor! To this Echeandía's only reply was the Spanish equivalent of "Shut up!" The soldiers then shoved the offender off to prison.

When the cell door closed upon him, he "never expected to see the sun rise and set again." Yet it is clear that Echeandía, for all his cruelties, was less of an oppressor than his victim supposed. Otherwise, surely Jim never would have looked upon the sun again.

It may be that the captive's revolt was highly inconvenient for Echeandía—more so than the rebel could have realized. The official, in preparing his papers and reports for the central government, may have been handicapped, if not embarrassed, since no other suitable translator was at hand. And this may in part account for the vehemence of his anger, which made him stoop to striking his prisoner.

As for Jim, he was paying the price of his revolt, even though less of a price than he had expected. For a week he remained in solitary confinement, without even seeing Señorita Peak, whom he declares, perhaps with some understatement, "was so justly dear" to his heart. As a further sign of the disfavor into which he had fallen, he had nothing to eat except corn boiled in rancid fat, against which he had once bitterly protested.

At this point outside circumstances came to the rescue. The trial of Captain Bradshaw had begun, and a separate statement had to be taken from Bradshaw, the supercargo Rufus Perkins, and each member of the crew, all of whom were to be questioned by a Mexican. But it happened that none of them except the captain could speak Spanish. And the captain, for obvious reasons, would not be permitted to translate his own answers, nor to serve as interpreter for the crew. Who, therefore, would act the part?

Echeandía, evidently hard pressed to find an interpreter, mentioned to Bradshaw that Jim was capable of serving. But, he added, one might as well deal with the devil himself. Bradshaw, however, volunteered to approach the refractory youth; and the governor, doubtless for lack of any suitable substitute, gave his consent. The prisoner therefore had a visit from the seaman, who was greatly amused to learn of the recent brawl with the governor. Despite his resolve to do no more translating for Echeandía, Jim acceded to Bradshaw's request, for he was ready, he said, to do anything he could to oblige the captain.

And so once more he was ushered into the presence of his archenemy, who asked if he had changed his mind and was now willing to serve again. Disregarding a gibe from the translator, who, referring to Bradshaw, emphasized that he was always willing to do a favor for a "gentleman," Echeandía arranged for the hearings to begin at eight the next morning. Captain Bradshaw meanwhile, claiming that some of the crew were trying to have him condemned, had secretly asked Jim to make the testimony of the various men correspond as closely as possible. How far Jim complied we do not know, but he answered as equivocally as a diplomat: he would do anything he could "in honor."

For many days the inquiry continued, while Jim arduously translated bills of lading and other maritime documents. And after a time, emboldened, he again put an old question to the governor: might he and his comrades not have permission to go out and recover their buried furs? Doubtless he expected a peremptory refusal; instead, he received a qualified assent. As soon as the matter of Captain Bradshaw was disposed of, Echeandía would not only permit the men to set out after the furs, but would send soldiers to protect them from the Indians.

The catch was in the long wait. It was now the nineteenth of July, and in August the flood waters of the Colorado would cover the bottom lands, ruining the furs. Therefore it would be necessary to set out very soon. But Echeandía declared that it was impossible as yet to make arrangements.

Nine days later, when the depositions in the Bradshaw case had all been taken, Jim renewed his request. But Echeandía, like a wily old lawyer who always finds excuses for postponements, temporized and delayed. Nevertheless, in remarkable contrast to his old-time severity, he granted a request of Captain Bradshaw: that Jim be allowed to stay with him overnight on his vessel. On the way to the ship—which was completely novel to Jim and delighted him—he stopped at the house of Sergeant Peak and saw his sister. "She received me," says Jim, "with open arms, and manifested the most unequivocal delight."

Aboard the ship the temporarily freed man had ample opportunities to descant upon the cruelties of Echeandía, including the death of Sylvester, of which Bradshaw had been unaware, since he had been absent at Monterey ("Monte el Rey," Jim calls it). The captain now unbared a daring plan: if convicted, he would slip his anchors and do his best to escape from the harbor, even at the risk of being sunk by the guns of the fort. Would Jim accompany him in the daredevil effort? If so and if they got away, he could take passage with Bradshaw to Boston, where the captain would find him some suitable employment.

Here surely must have been a great temptation for one whose present prospects were limited to a prison cell. As for the danger of the attempted escape—this could hardly have deterred a man so used to extreme risks as Jim. Nevertheless, after thanking the captain, Jim refused the offer. He and his comrades, he explained, had suffered much together and had gone through many trials and risked their lives for one another; and he could not desert them now and leave them perhaps to suffer new hardships in prison as the price of his flight.

After a night passed on the ship and after breakfast at the home of Sergeant Peak and his sister, Jim returned to the governor's office, where he angered Echeandía by a request to visit his six fellow prisoners, and was ordered to be searched for hidden arms and thrown back into his cell. One can only surmise what else he said to drive Echeandía to his harsh new outburst.

Until the twenty-eighth of August he remained confined, and then was again called to Echeandía's office to translate some letters. "Señor, do you still wish to go for the furs?" asked the governor, when the translations had been made. But Jim replied that probably it was too late; by this time it was more than likely that all the furs had been spoiled by the waters of the Colorado. However, he would be glad to make sure, and in any case he and his comrades might regain their traps.

There was now apparently only one question to be answered. If the governor did let the prisoners go for the furs, and permitted them their arms for self-defense, what security could they give for their return?

Jim replied that he knew of no such security, but that in any case it would be impossible for the men to make so dangerous a journey without the protection of their arms.

Reflecting on this matter in prison, to which he had been returned for the night, Jim felt sure that Captain Bradshaw would serve as his security if asked (though one wonders how eagerly Echeandía would have accepted the bond of such a man). However, Jim realized that it would not be right to ask anyone for a guarantee:

> I knew the character of my companions, and was so well aware, how they would feel when all should be free once again, and well armed, that I dared not bind any one in security for us. Such had been the extent of the injuries we suffered, and so sweet is revenge, and so delightful liberty . . . that I was convinced that Mexico could not array force enough to bring us back alive. I foresaw that the general would send no more than ten or twelve soldiers with us. I knew that it would be no more than an amuse-

ment to rise upon them, take the horses for our own riding, flay some of them of their skins, to show that we knew how to inflict torture, and send the rest of them back to the general on foot.

By "the general" Jim, of course, means Echeandía.

In the morning the prisoner was permitted to walk the short distance to the governor's office without a guard, and even this small amount of liberty gave him a feeling of exultation. He refers to the distance as "fifty yards," which seems inconsistent with his previous statement that the door of Echeandía's office was "directly in front" of his prison grate. But either his own cell or Echeandía's office may have been changed in the interval, or the words "directly in front" may merely have implied that the office was in a straight line ahead, where it could be seen from Jim's cell.

"*Buenos días*, Don Santiago," the governor greeted him, courteously, as he motioned him to a seat. And he at once revealed his plans: the seven Americans would all be allowed to use their arms; they would be accompanied by fifteen soldiers; and they would be granted a week to exercise before setting out on the expedition.

Jim naturally was delighted at these concessions, and so were his six comrades, all of whom greeted one another like brothers after being released from their cells. "They looked," reports Jim, "more like persons emancipated from the prison of the grave, than human beings; and I am perfectly aware, that my specter-like visage must have been equally a spectacle to them."

But could it be that after all their sufferings they would actually be free men again? Hope springs up, if not eternally, at least so irresistibly in the breasts of most of us that doubtless they believed so. And certainly none of them foresaw the wicked trick that Echeandía was meditating.

For a week all went well, while the men were permitted to

walk about the port, accompanied by soldiers; their only confinement was at night, when they had to sleep in the guardhouse. Then one day the governor called for Jim and had him
sent with a soldier a distance of about thirty miles, where he
arranged with a priest to obtain the horses and mules necessary
for the expedition. These were to be rented at about twenty-
five cents each a day. So far, it seems, all was proceeding as
smoothly as optimism could have anticipated. The men were
delighted when Jim returned and announced the success of
his expedition, and they drew fresh joy from the governor's
statement that they might set out on the morning of September 6, and that the animals would be ready for an early start
on that day.

It was on the evening of the fifth that the thunderbolt
struck. Then once more the seven prisoners were summoned
to the office of the governor, who asked them how many days
they thought the expedition would take. This was, to be sure,
a matter of conjecture, but they answered as well as they could.
Echeandía then informed them that, after all, he could afford
no soldiers to go with them; but he did not say why he had
made this discovery so suddenly, and at the eleventh hour.

The Americans, of course, were perfectly willing to go without the soldiers. However, could they even for a moment
have imagined that so astute a man as their old enemy would
simply let them go, trammel-free, unguarded, and with no
security for their good faith?

"To insure your return," he notified them, "I shall retain
one of you as a hostage." And while this sentence fell like a
crash of doom, he pointed to Jim and announced that he
was the chosen man. He must stay in prison until the others
came back.

But what if the others did not come back? Then the
governor would be convinced that the men were all spies, as

he had suspected from the first. And in that case the hostage, being one of the spies, would be executed.

A dreadful silence descended as the men stared at one another "in the consternation of despair." One can almost hear their repressed mutterings, their oaths. Some of them swore that it would be better to give up the expedition than to leave Jim behind. Others stood mute and undecided. Jim himself, meanwhile, furious at the betrayal of their plans and feeling as if some evil fortune were bent on thwarting him at every point, turned to his comrades and begged them to go and not to consider him. He had nothing to fear, he pleaded, nothing to hope for, and nothing to lose but life. It would not benefit him if they remained, and if they did not leave, this would be held to be proof that they were all spies who had never meant to return, and all consequently would be condemned and convicted.

This reasoning may appear just a little specious, but it convinced the men. They decided to go, even without Jim; but they swore by everything they held sacred that if they lived, they would return. And Jim, trying to resign himself, said that if he had to die, he would as soon be buried beside his father as anywhere; however, he did not think that the law would permit him to be executed.

In the morning, just before they set out, his comrades came to bid him farewell through his cell bars. He repeats the words of the German immigrant, "as good hearted a fellow as ever lived," who took his hand, burst into tears, and said, "Goot by, Jim, if I ever does come back, I will bring an army mit me and take yours and your daddy's bones from dis tamned country, for it is worse as hell."

If this was meant to provoke laughter, it failed in its purpose. Evidently the man, for all his attempts to console Jim, did not concede him much chance of living.

A short while later the six trappers, mounted upon mules,

had gone on their way. They were armed only with Spanish muskets, which "when fired," Jim says, he "would almost as soon have stood before as behind." Considering that the small party, so poorly armed, had to pass through the land of several tribes of hostile Indians, he did not expect ever to see any of his friends again.

12

Smugglers, Fur Hunters, and Smallpox

"Obtain a guard of soldiers, Ensign! Go to the house of Sergeant Pico! There you will find Captain Bradshaw and his supercargo Rufus Perkins. Take them both prisoners!"

From behind a door where he sat waiting, Jim heard Echeandía fling these commands at Ensign Ramírez. A train of unforeseen circumstances had put him in a strange position: he had asked permission of the governor to go to the Picos' (or Peaks') for a change of clothes; and, having been set free for this purpose, he had found the captain and his supercargo at the Peaks' and had consented to take a note from Bradshaw to the governor. The latter, having received the note, had asked him to sit down for a few minutes and had gone into another room and sent for Ensign Ramírez. A short time later, while conversing with the ensign the governor drew close to the door, evidently forgetting Jim's presence on the opposite side. Hence Jim unintentionally overheard his orders.

The orders, however, were not all that he overheard. He

149

learned that he was to be sent to the captain with a message, asking him to wait an hour and a half at the Peaks' for the governor's reply to his note. During this hour and a half Ensign Ramírez would gather the corps of soldiers necessary to arrest Bradshaw and Perkins. Their detention would, incidentally, insure that the *Franklin* and its cargo would be confiscated by the Mexican government.

It is not hard to imagine Jim's thoughts when he was entrusted with the message for Bradshaw. The captain and Perkins, his good friends, were in danger; and, what was more, his own best chance of freedom rested with these two, since Perkins had volunteered to take a message for him to Jones, the consul at Oahu, the most important of the Hawaiian Islands, and through the consul's intervention Jim hoped to obtain his release. Motives of friendship therefore combined with self-interest as he rushed to the captain and supercargo and warned them of their peril.

Quite naturally, the threatened pair hastened away to their vessel before the arrival of the armed guard.

But Jim, having saved them from the overhanging blade, found that he had complicated his own position.

Ensign Ramírez, after going in vain for his expected prey, waved his sword at the prisoner as he passed his cell door on the way to the governor's office. "Oh, you traitor!" he cried. Evidently he knew well enough who had warned Bradshaw and Perkins.

Jim now regarded his predicament as desperate. His concern, he reports, was not only for himself but for his comrades, who, on their return from the trapping expedition, might be seized as sharers in his guilt and might all be executed. As for himself, he was resigned. "I could not expect to live," he tells us.

Summoned to the governor's office, he was ordered to stand near a large table at which several clerks were writing, and was asked whether he had heard the conversation between Echeandía and Ensign Ramírez. His answer was an evasion, to the effect that he had not known that there was a conversation between the ensign and the governor. The official then asked whether he had advised Bradshaw to escape to his vessel, and whether he knew the motives that had prompted Bradshaw's action; if the witness did not tell the truth, he would pay the penalty with his life. Jim says that "I regarded all this as no more than the threats of an old woman"—which is hardly consistent with his statement, made only a paragraph before, to the effect that he expected to die. In any case he was sent back to prison, still with the promise of a death sentence if found guilty.

A few days later, he records, Bradshaw slipped his cable and escaped from the harbor. Passing through a hail of cannon fire while sailing within two hundred yards of the fort, he replied so vigorously as to drive the Mexican cannoneers from their posts. The vessel was, however, damaged by three shots through her hull, as well as by the grapeshot which scraped her sides.

Such was Jim's account, which is confirmed in essentials by Bancroft in his *History of California* (Volume III). But Bancroft's narrative differs in some respects from Jim's. "Forty cannon-balls," the historian tells us, "were sent after the flying craft, with no apparent effect," while the officers and crew were "shouting their derision of the Mexican flag." But sometime later the French captain Dahaut-Cilly, meeting the vessel in the Hawaiian Islands, found that two cannon balls had entered the ship's hull and two had damaged the riggings, while Bradshaw himself had been wounded. This, of course, Jim could not have known. His statement that three shots had pierced the hull does not differ so widely from Bancroft's account as to be worthy of more than passing note.

Bancroft, however, makes a major point of the disparity in dates between the two stories: he states that the flight of the *Franklin* occurred on July 16, whereas the *Personal Narrative* gives the month as September. In a footnote Bancroft declares that "Pattie's statements as to the details of the departure are so positive, so erroneous, and yet so closely connected with the details of his own affairs, as to leave a doubt as to the accuracy of those details."

To me this seems like magnifying a mote into a mountain. The facts, as given by both Pattie and Bancroft, are that Bradshaw's escape occurred sometime during the period of Jim's imprisonment; that the captain had been under suspicion of smuggling and of breaking various Mexican laws; and that Jim had had the opportunity to converse with him on several occasions and learn of his plans. Under these circumstances it really matters little whether Bradshaw made his break for freedom in July or in September; and if Jim's recollection led him astray by two months, let us ask how many of us, after a year or two, can accurately recall the months in which various events in our lives occurred, when those events are not connected with some emotional upsurge or with an anniversary or other circumstance clearly fixing them in time.

It is, of course, possible that the narrator, following a normal human tendency, exaggerated the part that he had played in the escape of Captain Bradshaw. But there is nothing implausible in the story as he tells it, and lack of confirmation from other sources is not sufficient reason for rejecting Jim's statements. We have, to be sure, the fact that he mentions a conversation with Captain Bradshaw that, if Bradshaw escaped in July as Bancroft definitely states, could not have happened as reported, since it concerned the trappers who left in September to recover the buried furs. However, it may be that the conversation actually took place with some other person and, by a trick of memory, was transferred in Jim's mind to Captain Bradshaw.

But to take leave of Bradshaw. Whether his escape occurred before or after the departure of the six trappers, we need not doubt Jim's story that he was kept in jail pending the men's return. And no matter when Bradshaw had fled, Jim would hardly be treated more kindly because of the suspicion that he had helped the smuggler to elude justice. He was persecuted, he says, not only by the governor but by sadistic soldiers, who made frequent visits to his cell, with the information that his six comrades had deserted him, and that he would pay the penalty by being hung or else would serve as a target for sharpshooters or be burned alive. Even if he did not take these predictions at face value, he was "harassed and tormented."

But on the last day of September, the alleged deserters returned—that is, four of them returned. The other two, one of whom had married in New Mexico, had decided to risk death by starvation or from Indian arrows rather than go back to prison; and they had, therefore, set out afoot across the wilderness, though the chances of their emerging alive were far from good. The remaining four came back without the furs, which, as expected, had been ruined by the river floods; but they did bring the traps, which they sold as a means of paying the rental charges on the mules. One might suppose that Echeandía would have been incensed at the disappearance of two of the men and would have taken their defection as proof that they had been spies. And it may be that this actually was the conclusion he reached, for he had the other four thrown back into prison—a poor reward for their faithfulness in returning!

Jim, who need no longer fear execution as a hostage, had at least the satisfaction of knowing that Echeandía had not benefited from the quest for the furs. He expresses his feelings with unabashed frankness:

I was thankful that he had obtained nothing but the traps, which, as he knew no more how to use, than a blind horse, could be of no utility to him. This feeling may seem a poor gratification, but it was certainly a natural one.

If the feeling was "certainly a natural one," it was just as certainly no compensation for the sufferings of Jim and his companions. Now for months they were kept in prison, denied the visits of the charitable Miss Peak, and condemned again to the detested diet of beans or corn fried in spoiled tallow. It is hard to say how long they might not have remained in confinement, had it not been for a strange and grisly rescuer.

After a time alarming letters began to reach the governor. Smallpox—a scourge whose dire effects we in this vaccine-guarded age have almost forgotten—had begun to rage along the northern coast. Many victims had succumbed, and Echeandía, deluged with petitions for aid, could no nothing and began to fear that the plague would spread to San Diego.

But what had Jim and his comrades to do with all this? Fortunately a great deal—fortunately for them, as well as for many another beneficiary.

It happened that, amid the possessions of Sylvester Pattie, there had been a packet of medicine, which included some smallpox vaccine (the successful technique for which, though still in a rather crude stage, had been developed by Dr. Edward Jenner in 1798). One day in the course of some casual conversation the German trapper mentioned to one of the soldiers that Sylvester had possessed some vaccine and had inoculated some people at the copper mines. The soldier promptly informed Echeandía, who as promptly sent Sergeant Peak to ask Jim if he had any of the vaccine.

Yes, replied Jim, he did have some, and, what was more, he knew how to use it; in proof he showed his own right arm, on which there were scars of vaccination. However, he would inoculate no one—not even his friend Sergeant Peak—unless he and his comrades were given their liberty. But he did almost immediately relent with regard to the sergeant and his sister; having received Peak's promise of secrecy, he agreed to vaccinate them both (though he does not explain how he could act in the case of the sister, whom at this time he was not permitted to see). As to vaccinating other people, he remained adamant, since his object was to "influence the fears" of the governor—this, he thought, represented his only chance of being set free.

Never before during his term of imprisonment had Jim been favored by such rapid action as when he sent Sergeant Peak to the governor with his proposal to vaccinate everyone possible in exchange for the freedom of his four remaining comrades and himself. Within half an hour, the sergeant returned—returned "bright with delight" at Echeandía's offer. If Jim would vaccinate people up and down the coast and conduct himself well in other ways, he would be given a passport for a year, at the end of which he would be paid for his services and receive his liberty.

Here certainly would seem to be an inviting proposition—and one which most men in Jim's position would have grasped. But to the sergeant's astonishment, the prisoner refused. He held to his original conditions—nothing would suffice except the assurance of liberty not only for him but for his comrades. More than that! He would make no agreement except in a personal interview with the governor.

Gloomily the sergeant tried to argue with him—to convince him that Echeandía would never accept such an ultimatum, and that he was courting some extreme punishment, possibly death itself. But whether out of weariness with life or in mere bravado, Jim said that in the present circumstances he did not fear death.

There being nothing else to do, Peak returned to Echeandía with Jim's ultimatum. And a few minutes later Jim was led once more to the office of his old enemy. The governor greeted him with some questions about the efficacy of the vaccine, repeated the offer he had made through Sergeant Peak, and, receiving Jim's refusal, gruffly asked what his terms were. Jim's answer, though we do not have the exact words, was such as to drive the official into a fury. Calling Jim a devil, he said that he would compel his obedience under pain of death. But Jim defiantly maintained that he would suffer any pangs that "His Excellency's" ingenuity could devise rather than go free while his comrades remained in jail.

Thereupon Echeandía delivered an ultimatum of his own. Jim would have twenty-four hours in which to think things over and accept the governor's offer or suffer the consequences.

At this impasse, clearly, each man thought himself wholly in the right. And yet, as so often in the case of a violent clash of wills, it is possible to see merit in both sides. From Jim's point of view, he was only standing by the comrades who had stood by him—the four stanch friends who had returned from the trapping expedition in order to save him from execution, although they might have remained away like their two defecting fellows, and perhaps even now be free on the open plains instead of moping in their solitary cells in unjust confinement. To accept his liberty while they were still imprisoned—and imprisoned for his sake!—would in Jim's mind have been base ingratitude and betrayal. The fact that, by refusing to inoculate the people of the coast he might be responsible for the death of many innocents, probably never entered his head—at least, not as a factor in his decision, which was obviously emotional rather than reasoned, and doubtless appeared brave and even noble in his own eyes.

But from Echeandía's point of view, nothing could have been more abominable, nothing more criminal than Jim's recalcitrance. Here was a man who had the opportunity to save lives and relieve the dire peril afflicting most of the coast. He had been offered generous terms—his release for a year, payment for his services, and eventual freedom. Yet the conscienceless rogue had the effrontery to defy the governor, refuse his reasonable offer, try to dictate to the government itself, and demand the liberty of four fellow ruffians who might break loose upon the people like a scourge. How Echeandía must have glowered, clenched his fists, and muttered oaths!

On the way back to his cell Jim was advised by the soldiers to accede to the governor's terms, the more so as the official was "a terrible man when enraged." But in the morning he had still not changed his mind. Summoned back to Echeandía's office, he was asked what security he could give for the good conduct of his comrades and himself if they were released on parole for a year; and he replied that, being unknown in the district, he could give no security. Something about this response further infuriated the governor. "*Carracho pícaro!*" he growled, along with other wrathful epithets. The dirty dog might lie and rot in prison!

But in the face of this outburst Jim perceived that the governor "was not inflexible in his resolution." The grounds for this conclusion are not evident; one might suppose that, in this conflict between two men of apparently unbending wills, the governor in his seat of power held all the trump cards. Jim, however, had a grim ally, and one not at all susceptible to the authority of the government. The smallpox still was spreading. During the following night Echeandía received word of the illness of many of his priests and the death of one; and terror, more powerful than anger or pride, now controlled his hand. In the morning Jim was summoned back to the office and, in what was apparently a mere face-saving move, was asked to produce the papers showing his father's commission as a ranger and his discharge from the service. Having obtained these from Miss Peak's and listened to Jim's translation of the documents, Echeandía reached a conclusion he could obviously have arrived at long before: that there was sufficient proof that Jim was an American.

But could Jim's comrades produce similar proofs? If they could, this would be all the governor required, as all Americans were permitted to go free. Strange that he had seemingly not known this before! But as if in self-justification, he explained that he himself would be responsible to the law should he release the men without being sure that they actually were Americans.

Now began a solemn farce, which surely could not have deceived so astute a man as Echeandía, and one ordinarily so skeptical. The four other prisoners—all long-bearded, haggard, and gaunt—were summoned before him and asked if they could show any papers proving that they were Americans. Each of them drew forth some "old black papers," which, for all we know, may have been receipts for the purchase of boots or bills for debts owed. No matter, however! Jim translated them to prove just what he wanted to prove—and the governor, not questioning his interpretations, agreed to let all the men out on trial for a week before granting them parole. During the seven days of grace Jim was to vaccinate all the people in the fort; while the men, who would still sleep each night in the guardhouse, would try to find some work that would give them bread and meat.

However, a knife blade still dangled over their heads. None of them could know at what moment some whim of the governor's might not clap them back into jail.

13

Adventures of an Amateur Physician

LIKE WILD animals escaped from their cages, the five men looked about them for ways to change their "freedom on trial" to permanent liberty. How could they save themselves from being, as Jim puts it, crunched "in the lion's jaw"? The first thing that occurred to them was that they must have weapons. If they could but get their rifles back, they would die before giving them up again! "The only difficulty now," Jim reports with naive understatement, "was to lay hands upon our arms." To this end, strategy would be of more avail than force, which they were in no position to exert; and in their eagerness to stay free they showed no more scruples than might be expected of cats who see their chance to claw their way out of a cage.

Had the weapons been in the hands of a stern and hostile guard, their prospects of regaining them would have been remote. But the officer in charge, as it happened, was "one of the best hearted Spaniards" Jim had ever seen. He must also

have been one of the most childishly trustful of Spaniards, or
Mexicans, for even a ten-year-old might have known that men
in the state of mind of Jim and his comrades would not volun-
tarily relinquish their guns once they had laid hands on them.
On the pretext that they wanted the arms for only a few minutes in order to clean them, Jim "appealed to his goodness of
heart." The man thought for a while, then replied that the
governor would punish him if he acceded to Jim's request
and were caught. But Jim, not hesitating at any promises
whatever, answered that there was no possibility that the
guard's kindness would be known to anyone; and—just in case
the man's "goodness of heart" needed some bolstering—he
supported his argument with a gift of ten silver dollars received
from Captain Bradshaw. This logic proved irresistible; the
rifles and pistols and also some ammunition made their way to
Jim through a back door, along with sundry words of caution.

With an elation easily to be imagined, Jim rejoined his
comrades, and the five men entered an empty old house, where
they put the weapons in order. Never again would they give
them up! "We had been so treacherously dealt with by these
people," he explains, "that we did not consider it any great
breach of honour to fail in our purpose of returning the arms,
particularly as the officer had taken my money." This reasoning was probably more convincing to Jim than it will be to
the reader, since the victim of his deliberate lies, though unable
to resist the temptation of ten dollars, had not treated him
treacherously. Moreover, Jim had been equally bent on de-
ceiving him, whether or not he accepted the money.

Since they could not walk around with the rifles, they hid
these in a thicket, while secreting the pistols inside their
clothes. Thus protected, they returned at night to the guardhouse, where they were visited by the officer who had given
them the weapons. Still naively supposing that they intended
to return the guns, he asked why they had not kept their

promise. One falsehood prompts another. Jim did not hesitate to say he would make good his word on the following morning, "thinking as before, that it made no great difference what is said to such persons, in a position like ours."

The morning was to involve them in fresh adventures. They met an American whose name Jim gives as James Lang, though Bancroft refers to him as Charles Lang. He claimed to be a colonizer but, according to Bancroft, was subsequently arrested after having been found in possession of dry goods, a barrel organ, and other articles "better adapted to smuggling than to colonization." Jim's story coincides with Bancroft's in that he states that the man had come to the coast in order to smuggle, as well as to kill sea otters for their valuable skins. He was now in the act of making secret inquiries about these animals and said that he had a boat and crew about eighty miles down the coast. Would not Jim and his comrades accompany him? If so, Lang would supply them with all necessary equipment, give them half of the catch, and eventually, after a visit to the Galapagos Islands, would provide them a free passage back to the United States.

The five men were willing to terminate their "freedom on trial" by accepting this offer. They picked a day on which to meet Lang at the settlement of Todos Santos, some distance down the coast; then consulted one another as to the best way to avoid falling afoul of the law in the event of detection. Because they must not attract attention, they could not use horses; and for the same reason they must leave at night. But the prospects, under these circumstances, did not seem too inviting; and three out of Jim's four companions, on a gust of cautious afterthought, reversed themselves and decided against the adventure. Would it not be better, they asked, to see the governor and request that they be allowed to go hunting, since they were now barefooted and needed some deerskin for moccasins? The only astonishing thing about such a request was the assumption behind it: that Echeandía might conceivably grant permission.

Naturally he did not grant permission. Therefore Jim and a companion, holding to their original scheme, set off together at twelve o'clock on Christmas night—a strategic time, since the people were all in church. They thus made good their escape and, traveling entirely by night, reached Todos Santos within seventy-two hours. But there a sharp disappointment awaited them. Captain Lang, instead of keeping his appointment with them, had had an undesired rendezvous with the Mexican authorities, who had taken his boat and arrested him and all his men on a charge of smuggling.

Fortunately the two fugitives were able to obtain this information without exposing themselves or coming out of the woods. Being famished, they applied at a house, where a widow and her two daughters gave them bread, milk, and cheese and lodged them for a week, while they awaited news of a vessel on which to flee the coast. But no vessel arrived.

They had now no choice but to return to San Diego, where they expected to learn that their three companions were in jail. Never again, however, would they surrender their own liberty!

Upon reaching San Diego, they found to their surprise that the three men were still at large, though the officer who had given them their arms was under arrest. Jim's remorse at his benefactor's detention is evident in his words, which are in no way consistent with his previous remarks on the subject, though it is equally evident that he would not have acted one whit differently if faced again with the same circumstances: "I had deceived the unfortunate man, when he had intended to do me a kindness, of the utmost importance to my interests, as I viewed it. He would probably be severely punished."

But what of Jim and the companion of his adventures? Would they, too, not be severely punished? They may well have asked themselves this question, for the governor, they were told, was "exceedingly anxious" for their return.

Having steeled themselves for the ordeal, the truants paid Echeandía a visit. They had first hidden their rifles, but they carried their pistols concealed on their persons, for they "were determined not to be taken to prison without offering resistance." Indeed, they were prepared to give their lives rather than go back to their cells; they could hardly hope to survive a battle with a corps of soldiers. And it would not have availed them to survive, since if they were disarmed and taken alive, perhaps after wounding or killing some of the guards, they could not have expected any fate better than execution.

Echeandía, who had had good reason to fear that he would never see them again, was surprised at their visit. Where had they been? "Upon a hunting expedition," answered Jim. But did they not realize that they had no right to go off without letting the governor know? Yes, they did realize, but they had asked permission, and it had been refused.

If Echeandía was enraged at this response, Jim does not mention the fact. But apparently the governor had his own reasons for not showing too much indignation. His next question was about the weapons: how had the two runaways obtained them? To this inquiry Jim made a truthful answer. Surely he realized that his only hope lay in telling the truth, since the governor, having arrested the man who gave them the arms, already knew what had happened.

But the two men, as Echeandía pointed out, had promised to return the arms—and why had they not done so? Again Jim took refuge in the truth: they had never intended to return them and would not give them up while they lived.

Had the governor been in a truculent mood, this blast of defiance might have led to a violent scene, with disastrous and perhaps fatal results. As it was, however, the official merely smiled and denied any interest in the arms. There was something of much greater importance in his mind; he had need of Jim and did not wish him killed in any foolish scuffle; the smallpox was still spreading on the coast, and it was necessary to vaccinate as many people as possible.

Now began a strange new phase of life for Jim. Within about four weeks he had inoculated all the people of the fort and all the Indians of the Mission of San Diego, three miles to the north. Then, having obtained a sufficiency of vaccine, though he does not say from what source, he was ready to range far afield. As a preliminary he and his four comrades were all released on parole for a year—which was by no means the same as complete liberty, since at the year's end they might all be clapped back into jail at a word from the governor. However, a year is a long time—at least, in anticipation and when one is young. The prospect of freedom for a full twelve months was so delightful that Jim "concluded to trust in Providence, and the generosity of the stranger, and think no more of the matter."

Before leaving on his travels he received a letter from the governor to the priests at the various missions, informing them that he was to vaccinate all the people, and ordering them to supply him with all necessary food and horses. In addition, he was to receive compensation for his services, though the amount was to be left to the people among whom he traveled—which was equivalent, he thought, to saying that he was not to be paid at all. However, an old priest at the Mission of St. Luis advised him to take certificates from the priests at each mission, mentioning the services he had performed; at the northernmost mission he would be compensated for all his services by one of the high dignitaries of the Church.

But after all, what could compensation in money matter beside the great, the overwhelming fact that he was free?

Concerning the trip that followed, Bancroft remarks in a

footnote that, "Strangely enough, there is no record in the archives concerning the ravages of small-pox or Pattie's professional tour; yet his statement is confirmed by the fact that the statistical tables show an extraordinary number of deaths this year among the Indians of the northern missions." Pattie's story is further confirmed by his specific reports concerning his travels, which, even though often less explicit than one could wish and though subject to minor inaccuracies, were such as no one could conceivably have made without visiting the places he describes.

From mission to mission he traveled, gaining revealing glimpses of Spanish California—that vanished California which has been described by historians as a land of Arcadian benignness and simplicity, where hospitality was the rule and want was unknown amid the generous wide spaces of a land largely given up to cattle raising. The narrator, though he could not linger long anywhere, depicts something of the life of the missions beneath the paternalistic rule of the padres.

He tells, for example, how at San Luis the priests were the governors and financial directors no less than the spiritual preceptors. It was they who handled all the income of the community; it was they who dispensed food and clothing; it was they who acted as guardians and, in a sense, as jailors of the women, locking up at night all those whose husbands were away and all young girls above the age of nine, while by day they entrusted their charges to the care of matrons— with results that appear to have been less than perfect, since Jim saw "women in irons for misconduct, and men in the stocks." And as if this supervision did not suffice, the priests appointed overseers to watch the Indians while they were at work—overseers who taught them such trades as carpentering, blacksmithing, and shoemaking, and were severe in their supervision, "applying the rod" to those who fell behind in their assigned labor.

"The greater part of these Indians," Jim relates, "were brought from their native mountains against their own inclinations, and by compulsion, and then baptised; which act was as little voluntary on their part as the former had been. After these preliminaries, they had been put to work, as converted."

Viewed in the light of such revelations, the Spanish Utopia appears just a little less Utopian. Forced labor is forced labor, whether performed beneath the whip of totalitarianism or under the rod of religion. It is probable, of course, that the good old padres, unable to see into the minds of the simple and freedom-loving natives, had persuaded themselves by pious rationalizations that they were justified in everything they did, since it was for the welfare of the souls of the people. And it is equally probable that few if any of them could foresee the time, not many generations distant, when most of the Indians of California would be no more.

Jim next visited the Mission of San Juan Capistrano, in present-day Orange County, southeast of Los Angeles; and there he found that an earthquake had shattered the church and killed twenty or thirty Indians. Having vaccinated six hundred people, he proceeded to the Mission of San Gabriel, where he vaccinated nine hundred and sixty; then on to "the town of the Angels," a small settlement whose flat-roofed houses, covered with bitumen, scarcely foreshadowed the thronged metropolis of the following century. After leaving Los Angeles he vaccinated close to two thousand Indians at the missions of San Fernando and San Buenaventura; stopped at the fort of Santa Barbara, where he went aboard several vessels and enjoyed the company of the skippers; then pressed on to San Luis Obispo and to Monterey, at that time the capital of Upper California, though Governor Echeandía preferred to make his headquarters at San Diego. The region was then covered with thick forests of pine and live oak, the haunts of large numbers of bears, which often attacked human beings.

In June 1829, having inoculated a total of twenty-two thousand persons, Jim reached the port of San Francisco. One could wish that he had left us some description of the place, but all that he mentions is that he saw the high church dignitary whom he had been advised to visit and presented him with the certificates of the priests in the various missions, and the letter from the governor. This prelate, whom Jim names as John Cabortes and whom Bancroft identifies as Padre Juan Cabot, asked him to remain in the vicinity for a week or two while he decided what compensation to make for his services.

In order to fill the interval, the visitor crossed the bay in the company of two Indians, in a craft made of the skin of sea lions, which they ordinarily used to hunt sea otters. The width of the bay, he reports, is three miles—which is fairly accurate for the crossing at certain points. Of the magnificent bay itself he says nothing, except that it is formed "by the entrance of a considerable river, called by the Spaniards Río de San Francisco" (evidently the Sacramento and the San Joaquin). Perhaps it was his bad luck to encounter one of those foggy days that so frequently visit the area at this season, cutting off the breathtaking views.

Reaching present-day Marin County, which is still largely covered with forests of redwood, Douglas fir, and live oak, he passed through "a beautiful country, with a rich soil, well watered and timbered," though these words convey no impression at all of the distinctive character of the region. After a journey of about thirty miles he reached Fort Ross, established in 1812 by the Russian Fur Company, and saw a man named Don Seraldo, whom he describes as the commander and whom he had met sometime before while vaccinating the people of San Diego. Seraldo accompanied the newcomer about the district, whose natural features greatly impressed him, though one is puzzled by his reference to "a lofty mountain . . . glittering with perpetual ice and snow."

None of the mountains in this vicinity glitter "with perpetual ice and snow," even if some of them have fugitive snow crowns at rare intervals in the winter. This, however, was the month of June. Could it be that the white cloud wreaths that sometimes linger about the peaks were mistaken by the observer for snow?

After a week at the fort Jim received a hundred dollars from Seraldo for his services, then returned to the port of San Francisco, where John Cabortes (or Cabot) wanted to know where he had been, and proceeded to put some telltale questions. How did he like California? What would he think of the idea of living here? To these queries Jim replied that he "very much admired the appearance of the country," and that he would enjoy living here under any other form of government; but he was careful not to say just what there was that he disliked in the present government. Cabortes then handed him a surprising document, which the recipient translates as follows:

I certify, that James O. Pattie has vaccinated all the Indians and whites on this coast, and to recompense him for the same, I give the same James O. Pattie my obligation for one thousand head of cattle, and land to pasture them; that is, 500 cows and 500 mules. This he is to receive after he becomes a Catholic, and a subject of this government. Given at the mission of St. Francisco on the 8th of July, in the year 1829.

JOHN CABORTES

14

Revolution

IF THE adventurer's thoughts had been centered on fabulous dreams of wealth, where could he have found more alluring prospects than Cabortes held out to him? He had been offered abundant riches, the only riches that the country afforded, riches in land and in livestock. He might become a cattle baron, the free lord of wide and fruitful domains. He might establish a home, might marry some kind and attractive person such as Señorita Peak, might rise to a position of influence and honor, and might never again be faced with the nerve-racking, back-breaking necessity to force his way in a hostile world. True, he would have to make one or two concessions. He must vow allegiance to the Mexican government, and he must accept the Catholic religion. But little obstacles of religious faith and national fidelity have not stood in the way of many another self-seeker. And surely a man so hardened by experience as Jim Pattie would make light of these obstructions.

Such, however, did not turn out to be the case. Far from it! "I was struck dumb," he tells us. "My anger choked me." He felt outraged, defrauded. What an abominable thing that after all the good services he had performed, the priest should attach strings to the proffered payment! Strings requiring that he be untrue to his native country and to the creed of his father!

"You look displeased, señor," remarked the priest, while his supposed beneficiary stood glaring at him.

Jim, believing that Cabortes had the power to hang him if he were insulted, had discreetly resolved to hold back his feelings. But now, no longer able to restrain himself, he launched forth in a tirade that surprised the good father. He would rejoice, he explained, to be in a land where he was justly treated!

What did he mean, demanded Cabortes, by being justly treated? And Jim replied that he would be justly treated in a country where a man paid what he owed without adding any of his own whimsical desires.

But probably he would have had to look far in order to find a phrase more galling to his hearer than "whimsical desires." Here again there was a wide bridge of understanding to be crossed. From his own point of view, the padre was doubtless acting magnanimously in offering the stranger a thousand head of cattle along with land. True, he did attach the conditions that the recipient was to become a Catholic and a Mexican national, but this, too, was for the young man's benefit, his material advantage as well as the eternal gain of his soul, which would thus be redeemed from destruction. In every way he had reason to give thanks for the benefits extended. Instead, he replied with rude and outrageous accusations!

We do not know, of course, whether Cabortes could have been induced to negotiate; or whether, if he had received a diplomatic rejection instead of an insult, he might

not have modified his terms or made some counter offer that
could have given Jim at least part of what he desired. But the
young man's response, which had all the finesse of a charge by
a grizzly bear, precluded any such possibility. He did not
hesitate to tell Cabortes that, rather than "consent to be
adopted into the society and companionship of such a band
of murderers and robbers," he would "suffer death." Little
wonder that when he had thus given "honest and plain utterance" to his feelings, the priest in a fury ordered him out of
the house.

Fearing attack from some of Cabortes' followers, Jim immediately seized his rifle, which he had left outside the house.
Then, in dread of pursuit, he hastened away to a ranch, where
for three dollars he obtained a horse, on which he took the
road to fresh adventures.

At Monterey he made arrangements to embark on an American ship, but soon repented the action, for within an hour
of setting sail he became desperately seasick. For several
months, however, he remained on the waters, enjoying excellent health upon his recovery from the seasickness; and
after visiting various ports (which he does not name), he
returned to Monterey, where he received some exciting news.
A revolution had broken out! A revolution against the rule of
Governor Echeandía!

The leader of the revolution was Joaquín Solis, who (though
Jim does not mention and probably did not know the fact)
was a convict whom the Mexican authorities had sentenced
to exile in California in punishment for some brutal crimes,
for which he would have paid a heavier penalty had it not
been for the part he had played in the war of independence
against Spain. There was, as Bancroft brings out, no need
for an uprising such as that of Solis, which was inspired in
large part by the efforts of an accused official named Herrera
to redeem his wrongs, and was aided by soldiers who in

general had no higher object than to collect overdue pay. In any event, the forces of Solis did take the presidio at Monterey without any trouble on the night of November 12, 1829, and threatened to spread their conquests to many other points.

Jim, upon learning of the revolution, was told of a promise by the rebel leaders: English and American traders would thenceforth have the same privileges along the coast as Mexican citizens—that is, if they aided the revolution with their advice and money. But less because of this practical consideration than because of his hatred of Governor Echeandía, Jim was delighted to learn of the revolt. "I do not know," he candidly proceeds, "if the feeling be not wrong; but I instantly thought of the unspeakable pleasure I should enjoy at seeing the general, who had imprisoned me, and treated me so little like a man and a Christian, in fetters himself."

Dominated by such revengeful dreams, he gave a portion of his small reserves to the revolutionaries and was only deterred by the advice of fellow Americans from offering his services as a combatant, "in hopes to have one shot at the general." Meanwhile (though there are some inaccuracies in Jim's statements concerning dates), Solis had made a march to San Francisco, but one that can hardly be called a military expedition, since he was nowhere opposed and at San Francisco the garrison gave him an artillery salute and immediately went over to his side. Observers saw reason to suppose that within a few months the entire coast would be under his command.

It was now Solis' intention to turn south and capture Santa Barbara. Yet actually the insurrection was much less formidable than might have appeared upon the surface. "Thus far," comments Bancroft, "all went well; but the leader had no ability, no control over his men; the army had no element of coherence, and would fall apart of its own weight at the slightest obstacle; yet if success should take the form of a hole, the fragments might fall into it."

As to the severity of the engagements indulged in by Solis, all observers agree. Jim tells of an encounter lasting three days, in which the only loss sustained by Solis was one horse. With perhaps some picturesque exaggeration, he repeats the story related to him: that "the cannon balls discharged from the fort upon the enemy were discharged with so little force, that persons arrested them in their course, without sustaining any injury." This is not far in spirit from the report of a Dr. Anderson, as quoted by Bancroft: "The two parties were in sight of each other for nearly two days, and exchanged shots, but at such a distance that there was no chance of my assistance being needed.

"All my original witnesses," adds Bancroft, "state that cannon were fired, but give no particulars save the important one that nobody was hurt." In this comic-opera war "safety first" was evidently the motto.

Meanwhile the leader of the teapot revolution, puffed up with victory, began to strut in the way of many another man whose self-esteem has suddenly become larger than his head. Whereas previously he had catered to the Americans, whose aid he had needed, now he bristled and began to threaten that he would put them in their place once he had the country under his thumb; he would compel them to swear allegiance to him, or be driven from the land. Such, at least, was the information brought to the Americans by Encarnación, the Mexican wife of Captain John B. R. Cooper, a former Massachusetts skipper who had settled in Monterey as a merchant.

The Americans, who did not receive the warning until after Solis had left Monterey, were alarmed. They consulted as to ways of thwarting their former ally, and reached a conclusion that in Jim's case represented one of those ironies that often make such a ludicrous tangle of human affairs. In view of Jim's attitude toward Governor Echeandía, nothing would seem more improbable than that he would hold out a helping hand to that official and strive to prevent him from being unseated. Yet this about-face, according to his own statement, is precisely what he made.

He was, he claims, one of a group of foreigners who sent a letter of warning to Echeandía (whose name he misspells "Echedio"). A runner was dispatched, along with two good horses and instructions about how to pass the army of Solis undetected in the night. It was while impatiently awaiting the results that Jim learned of the engagement, already mentioned, in which the only casualty after three days of fighting was one horse. This brilliant triumph caused the name of Solis to be—temporarily—exalted by his admirers until it seemed to shine among the fixed stars. Meanwhile the Americans, Scotch, Irish, English, and Germans at Monterey—a total of thirty-nine men—formed themselves into a military company under the command of Captain Cooper; and, having shut the people of the vicinity up in the fort at night so that they could not send informers to the enemy, they prepared for the return of General Solis.

To this extent the story as told in the *Personal Narrative* agrees with the report of Bancroft, who says that the recapture of Monterey was accomplished "largely by the aid of the foreign residents." But certain points in the two versions are more difficult to reconcile. One would not know from reading the *Personal Narrative* that Solis had been routed near Santa Barbara, after performing in typical style by announcing grandiloquently that his men would never surrender—and then almost immediately taking flight. But Bancroft tells us that the stragglers from the defeated army came trailing into Monterey, where they joined the garrison of their one-time enemies; and he also recounts that patrols were sent out to find the missing ringleaders. At this point there is some consistency between Jim's and Bancroft's accounts, along with many inconsistencies. Both writers agree that a contingent was sent out to capture Solis, but Bancroft tells us that the capture was made by a company of thirty under Antonio Avila, one of Solis' own convict companions; while Pattie offers a much more colorful tale, naming Captain Cooper as the leader and including himself as one of the chief actors. (Whether it is true or not that Cooper was the leader, we do know from the testimony of a Meliton Soto that Cooper's house was the headquarters of the anti-Solis forces.)

In any event, Jim reports that he was named as orderly sergeant in the final pursuit of Solis by a band of six horsemen, which, in the best style later to be made popular in motion picture western thrillers, dashed at full speed after the fugitives, exchanged shots with them, unseated six of them from their horses and disarmed them, and engaged in a duel with the seventh, who was knocked out of his saddle with four bullets through his body. With the corraling of the dismounted six, the act of surrender was made complete. "General Solis," says Jim, " offered me his sword. I refused it, but told him, that himself and his officers must accompany me in my return to the fort. He consented to this with a countenance so expressive of dejection, that I pitied him, notwithstanding I knew him to be a bad man, and destitute of all principle."

In his comment upon this passage Bancroft is almost savage. "There is apparently deliberate falsehood," he charges, "respecting his personal exploits in the capture of Solis." This, however, is a point on which it is impossible to pass an assured verdict. It is highly probable that there was some exaggeration in Jim's attempt to make himself appear a hero; one must take with at least a spoonful of salt the statement that it was he who was offered the sword of General Solis. But just to what extent was the presumed exaggeration deliberate? Let this be decided by those psychologists who have plumbed the full depths of human self-deception and understand the tendency of men to dupe themselves with the rose wreaths of their own fables. Amid the mists of a past whose details are insufficiently recorded, it is impossible to see all the facts with a crystalline clarity. Yet there is nothing basically improbable in Jim's statement that he was one of the party sent in pursuit of Solis. And we know that a man of his type, reckless and adventurous by nature and eager for action at all costs, would have been just the sort to volunteer for the exploit. "I wanted to have a shot at the fugitive," he tells us, "and took pleasure in the pursuit." Is there any reason to doubt that this expresses the literal truth? And whether Solis offered his sword to Jim or to some other captor, we have no evidence that Jim was not, as he claims, actually present to witness the death throes of the short-lived but colorful revolution.

15

The End of an Odyssey

If Jim was surprised at the irony that had put his name on the list of Echeandía's supporters, Echeandía was no less astonished to see Jim's name on that list. A truce now settled down between the two old enemies. The governor, upon coming to Monterey as an aftermath of the Solis affair, received a visit from the former prisoner, greeted him in a friendly way, confided that he had never expected to see him again, and inquired about his activities during the long period since they had last seen one another.

But new sources of irritation were not long in flaring up between the irreconcilable pair. Bristling at the governor's remark that he was glad to see his visitor a citizen of Mexico, Jim replied that neither was he a citizen nor would he ever consent to being one, and went on to proclaim that he preferred to be in a country where a man might come and go as he wished without being subject to inspection by every petty officer. This remark will seem the more out of place since

177

Jim has nowhere mentioned being subject to such inspection other than in his examination by Echeandía himself. And if he makes a poor score from the point of view of tact, he had nothing to gain in a practical way from the subsequent debate as to the advantages of freedom. One gathers from his own words that he even became threatening. Echeandía's "swarthy countenance grew pale," and Jim read in him a fear that his caller "might carry into execution the purposes of vengeance."

In this Jim may have been and probably was mistaken, for if Echeandía suspected any inclination toward violence he had only to speak a word in order to throw Jim back into prison. But apparently he was less fearful than puzzled, and perhaps was deeply troubled by this impulsive visitor, who expressed himself with such rudeness and at the same time with such deep emotion, and yet who had, paradoxically, been one of the very group of foreigners who had done their best to rescue the governor from the claws of the usurper Solis. What was one to do with such a man? When one offered him the best one had—citizenship in one's own beloved country—all he did was to dash it down like cold water!

Jim, for his part still aflame with resentment at his long imprisonment and at the privations that had led to the death of his father, had no desire to establish a cordial relationship with the governor. Why, then, had he come to see him? Because he wished a passport—a passport back to his own country via the city of Mexico. And if this might seem an unusual and roundabout route, there was an excellent reason— at least, in Jim's mind.

A short while before, he had had an interview with the United States consul John A. Jones, who had advised him to draw up an exact statement covering the length of his imprisonment and the value of the furs he had lost, and take this to the government in Mexico, asking to be indemnified for his loss, as well as for his unjust sufferings while in the guardhouse.

Looking back from our distance in time, this would seem to have presented no very promising prospect, for governments in those days were no more eager than governments are today to pay indemnities to obscure foreigners in compensation for problematical losses.

Jim, however, was sanguine and considered that "The probability of my success was not slight, provided I could establish the truth of my statement, by obtaining the testimony of those who were eye witnesses." He had, furthermore, been singularly favored by chance: a bystander, hearing his conversation with the consul and his remark that he had not the means to travel to Mexico City, had volunteered to defray the expenses, as well as the costs of the journey from Mexico back to the United States. After vowing to repay the generous stranger, Jim had made his decision to apply to Echeandía for a passport.

One might suppose that for a man who was hoping to extract a favor from the governor, Jim had not taken exactly the right track in opening the interview on an antagonistic note. Had Echeandía really been half as arbitrary and half as despotic as Jim supposed, the requested passport might have been refused—and what recourse would the applicant then have had? But Echeandía, feeling perhaps that it would be no loss to rid the country of such a troublesome sojourner, granted the passport readily enough. Upon being told why it was that Jim wished to visit Mexico City, he remarked, "You will not be able to recover anything, as I acted in conformity with the laws of my country." But then, showing a substratum of good will despite all the provocations of his visitor's speech and manner, he went on to promise, "If you will stay in this country I will give you something handsome to begin with."

Apparently Jim did not ask what he meant by "something handsome." He was not interested in anything "to begin with." If he could have extracted from Echeandía ten times the indemnity that he hoped to obtain in Mexico City, probably he would still have gone to Mexico City. In a way that was logically pointless but psychologically understandable, he went on to reproach Echeandía for his imprisonment and to imply that there was no law justifying him in having thrown the eight Americans into the guardhouse. If this outburst accomplished nothing else, at least it gave Jim the satisfaction of releasing his pent-up feelings.

The sailing was arranged for the ninth of May, 1830, on the *Volunteer*. In this respect Jim's account agrees in detail with Bancroft's, who also mentions the *Volunteer* and gives May 8 as the day on which he boarded the ship prior to sailing. In the same vessel—and in this also Bancroft and the *Personal Narrative* are at one—Solis and some of the other political prisoners traveled in irons (Bancroft adds that they were subsequently released without further punishment). In a final interview with Echeandía on some passport matters, Jim and his old enemy seem to have been on a friendlier footing than on most occasions; Echeandía joked about the honor Jim would enjoy of traveling in the same ship with General Solis, and he replied with some appropriate witticism. Perhaps each was put in a good humor by the thought that he would never see the other again.

Just before the embarkation Jim had engaged in a variety of occupations. Along with a Portuguese companion, he had gone up and down the coast hunting sea otters, those once-abundant fur animals which have since been almost exterminated by the greed of the pelt-seekers; within ten days the pair had taken sixteen victims, whose skins even then sold for as high as seventy-five dollars each. By way of diversion at other times Jim had watched the so-called sport of bull-bear baiting, by which a bear and a bull were tied together in such a way that they could not separate; in the resulting conflict, which would no doubt have won applause in a Roman amphitheater, either the bear would be fatally gored or the bull would be torn to death. Jim likewise witnessed bullfights, a kindred form of sadistic recreation, which seems to have been enjoyed wherever the Spanish influence dominated.

During all this period apparently he saw nothing of the four remaining companions of his desert adventures, with whom, however, he claims to have been in constant correspondence. All that he now reports about them is that, having been freed on parole, they were "in the town of the Angels." But what they were doing in Los Angeles, and whether they remained there, and what eventually happened to them, he does not tell us (though from other sources we know that one of the men was Nathaniel Miguel Pryor, who settled in Los Angeles, where he was made a village councilor and died in 1850). Except for Pryor, the men are all shadows as they take their departure from the *Personal Narrative* and from history— without color or individuality, despite the stirring events that had checkered their lives.

Now that Jim was about to leave California perhaps forever, did he feel no regret? One suspects that he did. In a telling passage, in which he voices his dislike of the inhabitants and particularly of the priests, whom he accuses of holding the Indians brutally under their thumbs, he goes on to say that "this country is more calculated to charm the eye, than any one I have ever seen. Those, who traverse it, if they have any capability whatever of perceiving, and admiring the beautiful and sublime in scenery, must be constantly excited to wonder and praise."

In Mexico also he was to see some magnificent scenery. Having disembarked at San Blas, he made his way overland amid an armed company to Guadalajara—a journey of eight days. On passing through the villages, he was struck by the numbers of beggars, who asked alms not for themselves but in the names of the saints whose images they wore about their necks or wrists. From Guadalajara they pushed on to Mexico City, which they reached in another five days. And there Jim saw the American *chargé d'affaires*, Butler, who showed him an appeal from President Andrew Jackson to the President of Mexico, requesting him to release some Americans imprisoned in California (presumably this refers to members of the Pattie party, but on this point the *Personal Narrative* makes no express statement).

Accompanied by Butler, Jim visited the palace of the Mexican president in order to get a passport to Vera Cruz, from which he expected to take ship for the United States. He mentions that it was "a splendid building, although much shattered by the balls discharged at it by the former President Guerero [sic]" (a reference to the revolution of 1829, in which President Vicente Guerrero was deposed by the revolt of Vice-President Anastasio Bustamante, aided by most of the army). Whatever the means by which he had risen to power, Bustamante impressed Jim favorably. Receiving him in a room where several clerks were busily writing, he addressed his visitor courteously, manifested great interest in the fact that he had just come from California, and gave him his passport without difficulty.

Two points about the interview stand out. The first is an omission so glaring that one can only regard it as deliberate. Jim, according to his own statement, had come to Mexico with the object of seeking redress for his wrongs and losses. But now that his opportunity had arrived—now that he was face to face with the Mexican chief executive—apparently he said nothing whatever on the subject. Or if he did say anything, he fails to mention it in the *Personal Narrative*. One cannot believe that the neglect of this important topic, if indeed he did neglect it, was due to lack of courage; the man's entire recital makes it clear that he did not hesitate to express himself on any likely or unlikely occasion. A natural conclu-

sion, therefore, is that for some good reason he had reconsid-
ered the idea of discussing the subject with the president,
perhaps after the *chargé d'affaires* or some other informed
person had warned him of the uselessness of the attempt.
Knowing what we do of Jim's temper, we can be sure that if
he had broached the subject and been rebuffed, he would not
have written favorably of the president, and would have done
his best to evoke sympathy by telling of the unjust refusal. On
the other hand, if he had changed his mind about petitioning
the government for redress of his grievances, why does he not
mention the circumstances? This, one fears, must remain
among the permanent mysteries connected with the trials and
adventures of James Ohio Pattie.

The second point concerns Governor Echeandía. Upon
hearing Jim's account, the president remarked that the governor had violated the law in several particulars, and that, accordingly, he had been asked back to Mexico to answer for his
conduct. Jim took this to mean that Bustamante did not ap-
prove of Echeandía's treatment of the Americans. "I was
surprised," he states, "at the condescension of the President
in expressing to me any part of his intentions with regard to
such a person." This story, when checked with other sources,
has evident elements of truth, even though one cannot believe
that the detention of the Americans had anything to do with
Echeandía's loss of favor with the home government. The
facts, as made known by other authorities, are that on March
8, 1830 (several months before Jim's arrival in Mexico), Lieu-
tenant-Colonel Manuel Victoria had been appointed to suc-
ceed Echeandía; but the latter, having delayed transfer of the
command, joined a rebellion against the government in the
latter part of 1831 and succeeded in clinging to his rule until
the spring of 1833. It is interesting, in any case, to note that
Jim's archenemy—though for reasons that had nothing to do
with Jim or his comrades—was not to remain in control very

long after the departure of the man he had so antagonized and injured.

On the journey across the mountains from Mexico City to Vera Cruz, Jim ran into another of those adventures that crisscrossed his career. The traveling, in those days before railroads, was done by stagecoach, and there were eight in the conveyance, including the coachman and three women. The party was, accordingly, no match for a band of about fifty armed and mounted men, which surrounded them in mid-afternoon of the second day and announced that they were followers of the deposed President Guerrero. Not hesitating to combine banditry with politics, they proceeded to deprive the travelers of their weapons and of everything else they considered worth taking, though they did permit Jim to keep his trunk of clothing. The robbery completed, their attention was attracted to a Mexican officer who had been traveling in the coach beside his wife. Recognizing him as an enemy of Guerrero, they dragged him from his seat and expressed their political sentiments in the most decisive way, by hanging him in the presence of his wife. The coach was then ordered to drive on.

Jim says little more about this grisly affair, except that the bereaved woman was left at Xalapa in the care of some relations. The rest of the journey to Vera Cruz, which lasted another week, was evidently uneventful; and from that port Jim took ship for New Orleans. Lacking the passage money, he was given the sum by the United States consul, Stone, and some parties unnamed. "It was very painful to me," he confesses, "to incur this debt of gratitude, as I could not even venture to hope that it would be in my power to repay it." He goes on to describe his further thoughts as he sailed for his own country:

My dreams of success . . . were vanished forever. After all my
endurance of toil, hunger, thirst and imprisonment, after en-

countering the fiercest wild beasts in the desert, and fiercer men, after tracing streams before unmeasured and unvisited by any of my race to their source, over rugged and pathless mountains, subject to every species of danger, want and misery for seven years, it seemed hard to be indebted to charity . . . for the means of returning to my native land.

Doubtless there is here a degree of self-pity. And quite as certainly this account ignores the fact that Jim, had he set his mind on it, might have prospered in California (though it is a question whether he and the Mexican authorities would ever have harmonized). But his complaint is in any case a human one, with some justification in his grueling experiences, which had left him with nothing except an empty pocket and a weary heart and mind.

Approaching New Orleans, he let himself be soothed by nostalgic thoughts and became gently sentimental as his imagination ranged across the hundreds of miles of river separating him from his childhood home:

I cannot express the delight which thrilled and softened my heart, as I fancied myself entering my home; for it was the home I had known and loved when my mother lived. . . . There were my brothers and sisters, as I had been used to see them. The pleasant shade of the trees lay upon the turf before the door of our dwelling. The paths around were the same, over which I had so often bounded with the elastic step of childhood, enjoying a happy existence. Years and change have no place in such meditations.

But all this was mere daydreaming. At New Orleans he was faced with the hard, practical reality that he had not the money to pay his passage up the river. In order to obtain the required amount, he half agreed to accept an offer to return to Vera Cruz, where he would aid in disposing of a vessel and its cargo. But he was warned against this course by an Englishman named Perry, whom he had met aboard ship and who re-

minded him that he would be going back to the Mexican port
during the yellow fever season, and would probably succumb
to the disease. Perry offered financial aid, which Jim refused; he
had decided to run the risk at Vera Cruz rather than accept
assistance from a comparative stranger. But Perry, sincerely
concerned for the safety of his new-found friend, introduced
him to an influential American, J. S. Johnston, United States
Senator from Louisiana; and Johnston not only joined Perry
in arguing against a return to Vera Cruz, but offered to pay
Jim's passage up the river. The young man's compunctions
about accepting aid from a stranger were now subordinated to
his genuine need. He "thankfully" accepted the offer, though
he promised to repay Johnston as soon as he could—to which
the senator courteously replied that "it was a matter of no
consequence."

At Cincinnati he said goodbye to the philanthropic poli-
tician, from whom he had a letter of introduction to Timothy
Flint, the writer who was to offer his invaluable services in
editing the *Personal Narrative*. And now, approaching journey's end, Jim suddenly realized that he had no home at all; his
mother and father were dead, his brothers and sisters widely
scattered. When he actually did reach his destination, the
disillusionment was sharp and searing:

I have still before me . . . the picture of the abode of my infant
days and juvenile remembrances. But the present reality is all as
much changed, as my heart. I meet my neighbors, and school
fellows, as I approach the home of my grandfather. They neither
recognize me, nor I them. I look for the deep grove, so faithfully
remaining in my memory, and the stream that murmured
through it. The woods are levelled by the axe. The stream, no
longer protected by the deep shade, has almost run dry. A storm
has swept away the noble trees, that had been spared for shade.
The fruit trees are decayed.

He was met by his tottering old grandmother, to whose mind he only brought sorrowful memories of his father, dead in a far-off land. He "could scarcely have remembered" his grandfather, who, in a feeble and trembling voice, asked question after question about his son Sylvester. And he saw but one of all his brothers and sisters, and that one was too young to recognize him. At the home of a sister, whom he had last seen as a child and who was married to a stranger, he found a temporary home, where in a world-weary spirit he tried to "weave a new web of hopes, and form a new series of plans."

But the nature of his "new web of hopes" and of his "new series of plans" remains somewhat vague. Of his further career practically nothing is known. I have been able to find only two reports, both admittedly unreliable and mutually contradictory. The more substantial-sounding of the two proceeds from William Waldo, who in 1880 reported to the Missouri Historical Society some of his recollections of the fur trade of fifty years before and mentioned that James Pattie, upon returning from his western adventures, entered Augusta College, Kentucky. Nothing regarding Pattie, however, has been unearthed in the attempt to investigate this story, and his name has not been found in a list of one hundred and fifty-three graduates, which does not preclude the possibility that he was a student without graduating—the more so as the Pattie family is recalled to have lived within six miles of the college.

Whatever the facts as to Augusta College, Waldo continues in a tragic vein:

> This man left my camp in the Sierra Nevada Mountains, amidst the deep snows of the terrible winter of 1849–50; and his sister, whom I met in Missouri eleven years after, told me that was the last account she had ever received concerning him. I suppose he perished in the deep snow, or was killed by Indians.

The last sentence, of course, is sheer surmise, and the whole story is based upon the flimsy and unverified recollections of an old man. Yet it is not improbable that an adventurer of Pattie's type would be drawn to the Gold Rush of '49, though this does not necessarily mean that he lost his life as Waldo suggests.

As opposed to the above, I find a footnote in Bancroft—a statement tenuous, doubtful, and likewise worthless as historical evidence, yet implying that the saga of James Ohio Pattie may not have ended in the deep snows or beneath Indian arrows:

> *Letter in Vallejo, Doc. xxx, 85.* In 1883 a man whose name I cannot recall, apparently trustworthy, while visiting my library, stated that his wife was a niece of Pattie, and that the latter had spent some time at her residence in San Diego of late years, or at least since 1850. The man promised to obtain from his wife a more definite statement on the subject, but I have not received it.

Perhaps it is fitting that the afteryears of James Ohio Pattie should be lost amid the vast anonymity of history. The great period of his life, perhaps the only period worth remembering, had been the six years during which he had suffered the unspeakable hardships of desert and mountain pass and prison cell, enduring excruciating torments, facing untamed Indian tribes, engaging in bouts with wild beasts and wilder nature, threading his way through unknown river canyons, sinking from peaks of hope and courage to pits of depression, but still fighting on in a way that makes him typify the pioneer and the pathfinder of a vanished day and race.